W9-BZH-321

BREWERS ESSENTIAL

Everything You Need to Know
to Be a Real Fan!

Tom Haudricourt

TRIUMPH
BOOKS

Library of Congress Cataloging-in-Publication Data

Haudricourt, Tom, 1954–
    Brewers essential : everything you need to know to be a real fan! / Tom Haudricourt.
        p. cm.
    Includes bibliographical references.
    ISBN-13: 978-1-57243-947-4
    ISBN-10: 1-57243-947-5
    1. Milwaukee Brewers (Baseball team)—History. I. Title.

GV875.M53H38 2008
796.357'640977595—dc22
                                                                2008000460

This book is available in quantity at special discounts for your group or organization. For further information, contact:

Triumph Books
542 South Dearborn Street
Suite 750
Chicago, Illinois 60605
(312) 939-3330
Fax (312) 663-3557

Printed in U.S.A.
ISBN-13: 978-1-57243-947-4
Design by Patricia Frey

A lot is asked of the wife of a baseball writer. Up front, she knows her husband is going to be away for long periods of time throughout the summer, when regular folks are taking vacations, engaging in cookouts, and basically just kicking back. For the wife, there are sacrifices to be made, functions to be missed, and family business to be conducted over the telephone.

Living in Wisconsin, an additional dynamic comes into play. When the husband goes away to spring training, the wife is left behind to shovel snow, clear driveways, and coax the dogs to go out and do their business on frigid mornings when they have no inclination to do so. All the while, the husband tries not to mention that he is wearing shorts and a T-shirt and enjoying balmy weather in Arizona.

With all that in mind, I would have to be absolutely nuts not to dedicate this book to my wife. Being a "baseball widow" requires patience, understanding, and the knowledge that life is going to be a bit different from that of the average working stiff and his family. This book is for you, Trish. It's also dedicated to my parents, who are awfully proud to have a baseball writer for a son.

Contents

Foreword

If it wasn't for George Bamberger, I wouldn't have had a career. George gave me a chance to play when he took over as manager in 1978. He said, "You're my center fielder." I had waited for an opportunity to play every day, and he was the manager who gave it to me.

Really, I think the history of the Milwaukee Brewers started in 1978. That was when a bunch of castoffs and kids coming through the system were put in a mold by Bamberger and became winners. We won 93 games that season, and that's when the club took off. Prior to that, we were lucky to win 65 games a year. We really became a factor in '78, and it stayed that way all the way through 1982.

I think the fans grew to love me because of my style of play. I had a reckless abandon. I had waited for a number of years to play and I wasn't going to waste the opportunity. I'd run into walls. I broke up double plays hard. I ran every ball out. That's the way I played, and my numbers grew as I played more. I hit 32 home runs in '78, batting ninth in the lineup. Somebody asked me, "How does it feel, hitting ninth?" I said, "It's a hell of a lot better than hitting 10th."

We won a lot of games from 1978 through 1980, but somebody in the division always had a better season than us. If they had had the wild card back then, we would have been in the playoffs just about every year. We finally broke through in 1981 and got our first taste of the playoffs against the Yankees in that mini-series (after the strike-split season). We took them to five games and probably should have beaten them.

The next year, 1982, it all came together for us. There were a lot of intangibles on that team. We all got along well together. It's not like that on every team. Some teams have guys more into their own thing. We'd have 15 or 20 guys hang out together after games. On off days, we'd go fishing together or play golf together. It's hard to be around a bunch of guys every day and get along all the time, but we did.

We played hard together on the field, and won a bunch of games. The guys grew together and learned how to win, and we really cared for each other. We were like the Three Musketeers—one for all and all for one. I know that sounds corny, but it was true. We didn't have anybody with a huge ego who thought he was better than everybody else. We just didn't have that.

We came damn close to winning it all that year. We had a lot of guys banged up, we didn't have Rollie [Rollie Fingers, the team's stellar closer] at the end, but we still took the Cardinals to the seventh game of the World Series. It would have been fabulous to have won the World Series, but a lot of guys who make it to the Hall of Fame never do get the chance. I played with Hall of Famers such as Robin Yount, Fingers, Paul Molitor, and Don Sutton.

There's no doubt that playing for the Brewers was the highlight of my career. When I got traded to Cleveland, the game just wasn't fun anymore. It wasn't the same. The teams weren't as good. It was a crushing blow to be away from all the guys I played with in Milwaukee. I never understood it. Baseball became a job after that. That's all it was.

When I came back to Milwaukee with Cleveland, there was a big crowd and banners everywhere. That meant a lot to me. That was the only time I can actually remember being nervous. That was one of the most memorable nights of my career. The fans in Milwaukee were always great to me. I'll never forget that.

One of the last times I talked to Wendy Selig [former club president], she told me, "Gorman, you've always been a Brewer, and you'll always be a Brewer." I'm very proud to have played in Milwaukee, and I'm still proud to be recognized as a former Brewer. I had a wonderful career. To still have access to the organization and be out there with a Brewers cap on means everything to me. I'll be a Brewer until the day I die.

—Gorman Thomas

Few players, if any, who have worn a Milwaukee Brewers uniform have been more beloved by the team's fans than Gorman Thomas. A blue-collar player in a blue-collar town, the power-hitting center fielder went from being one of "Bambi's Bombers" to become a "Harvey's Wallbanger" in the late '70s and early '80s without missing a beat. Affectionately known as "Stormin' Gorman" due to his reckless style of play—both as a fielder and on the bases—Thomas hit more home runs from 1978 to 1982 than any other player in the American League. He came to love the city and its fans as much as they loved him, and he still maintains that the saddest day of his life was June 6, 1983, when he was traded from Milwaukee to Cleveland. Now working on a personal services contract for the club, Thomas can be found at Miller Park for nearly every homestand, a Brewers cap still on his head.

Acknowledgments

Except for a brief time in 2002 and 2003, I've covered the Milwaukee Brewers for a local newspaper since August 1985. The first 10 years were spent at the *Milwaukee Sentinel*, where we tried to beat the rival *Milwaukee Journal* on as many stories as possible. In 1995, while baseball was still on strike, the *Sentinel* and the *Journal* merged to form the one big, happy family known as the *Milwaukee Journal Sentinel.*

Accordingly, much of the archival research in putting this book together involved going back and reviewing stories that I had written about the team. But stories written by other staff writers, both before and after the merger—including Tom Flaherty, Drew Olson, Gary D'Amato, Frank Clines, and many, many others—also provided valuable information and quotes.

Some of the anecdotes and quotes in this book were taken directly from those articles. Many others were obtained by interviewing former Brewers, who told stories and shared the details of key moments in club history, many of which have not been published previously.

The story of the Brewers begins with the 1969 expansion Seattle Pilots, who moved to Milwaukee the following year. Much information about that turbulent time came from Internet research, stories in *The Seattle Times*, and books such as *The Seattle Pilots Story* by Carson Van Lindt and *The Lords of Baseball* by Harold Parrott, who worked in the club's front office.

It was also helpful to have each edition of the Brewers' media guide, published annually by the club's media relations department, at my disposal. Past club employees, such as Mario Ziino, who is as close as it gets to being the franchise historian, also pitched in with anecdotes and information that proved invaluable in putting together *Brewers Essential.*

It's impossible to name everyone who helped, but you know who you are. Many, many thanks.

Introduction

When the Brewers made it to the World Series in 1982, there was no way to know that they wouldn't get back, or even return to postseason play, until who knows when. Trying to end a 25-year drought, the 2007 Brewers led their division much of the year, only to fall two games short of their dreaded rivals, the Chicago Cubs.

The World Series–edition Brewers of '82 figured to be a powerhouse for years to come, but things quickly unraveled at the end of the '83 season. Manager Harvey Kuenn, heralded as the club's saving grace when he took over the reins the previous season, was fired. Players were injured, others got old, and still others were shipped off to other clubs.

What followed were mostly lean years. There were some breakthroughs under manager Tom Trebelhorn in the late '80s, when the team was competitive, including the marvelous "Team Streak" season of 1987. But the Brewers never returned to the top, and eventually management was overhauled.

There was a season to remember under new manager Phil Garner in 1992, when the Brewers pressed the eventual World Series champion Toronto Blue Jays to the wire. If only there had been a wild card in those days, the franchise's playoff drought could have been snapped.

A combination of small-market economics and bad baseball decisions caused the Brewers to stumble through the baseball wilderness over the next dozen years, with nary a winning record. They officially bottomed out in 2002 with a 56–106 finish, worst in franchise history. Yet another management overhaul took place and the club was later sold, ending 35 years of ownership by Bud Selig and his family.

That miserable stretch of losing finally ended in 2005, when the Brewers finished with an 81–81 record. Never had a .500 slate felt so good! To their credit, general manager Doug Melvin and manager Ned Yost came in and raised the bar internally, proclaiming that anything less than a playoff club would be considered a failure. In a lesser yet significant accomplishment, the '07 Brewers posted the franchise's first winning season in 15 years.

Without another playoff berth to cheer, long-suffering Brewers fans have reveled in the past, celebrating the '82 World Series team with a 20th-anniversary affair in 2002 and a 25th-anniversary tribute in 2007. Along the way, there were moments to cherish, such as the Hall of Fame inductions of Brewers stars Robin Yount and Paul Molitor.

But you can only live in the past for so long. The '07 Brewers teased their fans until the final weekend, providing hope that a breakthrough was just around the corner. People still talk about how wild the town was in October 1982. When the Brewers make the playoffs again, the celebration might go on for weeks, perhaps months. The fans are more than ready.

Hang a Right at Vegas

It all began on April Fool's Day.

When Judge Sidney Volinn slammed down his gavel on April 1, 1970, it certainly was no joke. Volinn ruled the Seattle Pilots were bankrupt and would be sold to a group in Milwaukee led by Bud Selig and Ed Fitzgerald.

And, just like that, the Brewers were born.

There was no time for passing around cigars or hearty slaps on the back in Cheeseville. With the start of the season less than a week away, the Pilots' equipment trucks had already left spring training in Tempe, Arizona, and headed for Las Vegas, where the drivers awaited word of the club's fate.

If the Pilots continued to exist, the trucks would be sent to Seattle. If the club was sold, they would head for Milwaukee.

The phone call came. The Pilots were dead and the Brewers were born. Off to Milwaukee the equipment went.

The next day, the banner headline in the *Milwaukee Journal* proclaimed: "We're Big League Again!"

With the season opener set for April 7 at home, there was no time to order new uniforms. The Pilots' name and logo were ripped off each jersey and "Brewers" was stitched on. An "M" was placed on the caps but the bills still had the Navy-inspired "scrambled eggs," giving the new team in the Midwest a bit of a nautical flavor.

Pilots first baseman Mike Hegan recalled the uncertain nature of spring training, as players tried to focus on daily drills while awaiting news from Seattle of the team's fate.

"One day, it looked good. The next day it looked bad," said Hegan, who would have preferred to stay in Seattle. "Every day, there was a different rumor. I thought we were going to stay. Then, one day they came in and told us we were moving to Milwaukee."

When the team arrived in Milwaukee late in the evening on Sunday, April 5, they were greeted like conquering heroes. In what amounted to an impromptu pep rally, several thousand eager fans were waiting at the airport when the team's flight landed, stunning players still trying to get used to the idea that they no longer were the Seattle Pilots.

"It was unbelievable," said Hegan. "There was never that kind of interest in Seattle. We were kind of shocked. None of us knew anything about Milwaukee. When we got to the airport, people were there with signs, ready to greet us."

On April 7, the fledgling Brewers—under the direction of manager Dave Bristol—took the field for the first time at County Stadium, which had remained fallow for the most part since the Milwaukee Braves bolted after the 1965 season for the supposed greener pastures of Atlanta. With sunny skies and temperatures in the 50s—Chamber of Commerce weather for Milwaukee at that time of year—37,237 fans filed through the turnstiles to welcome big-league baseball back to the city.

TRIVIA

Who was the Brewers' starting pitcher in the team's first game, which pitted them against the California Angels on April 7, 1970?

Answers to the trivia questions are on page 147.

Amid all the fanfare, the Brewers got off to an ignominious start, absorbing a 12–0 beating at the hands of the unimpressed California Angels.

"I tell people it was the only game that I didn't care if we won or lost," said Selig, who over the years became infamous for his temper tantrums in the owner's box at County Stadium when things didn't go the Brewers' way.

As for the remarkably short time the new owners had to get ready for the return of baseball to the city, Selig said, "I wouldn't want to go through that again. It was absolutely the six wildest days getting ready."

Fans trekked through inclement weather to buy season tickets. Workers furiously shoveled snow from the County Stadium grandstands.

Bud Selig, then-president of the Milwaukee Brewers, reads a telegram from American League President Joseph Cronin on April 1, 1970, regarding the move of the Seattle Pilots. Photo courtesy of AP/Wide World Photos.

If not for the determined and dogged efforts of Selig, the franchise shift never would have happened. Profoundly saddened and heartbroken when the Braves left town, he made it his life's mission to return Major League Baseball to Milwaukee.

Along the way, there were many disappointments. Selig pinned his hopes on expansion to get a big-league franchise, only to be hugely disappointed when Kansas City and Seattle (the irony would come later) were named as new American League hosts while Montreal and San Diego got the nod in the National League.

As a favor to Selig, John Allyn and his older brother, Arthur Allyn Jr., owners of the Chicago White Sox, played nine "home" games at County Stadium in 1968 and 11 more in 1969. Those games were highly successful, drawing much larger crowds than the Sox were getting at Comiskey Park.

3

Seeing how successful the White Sox were in drawing fans to County Stadium, a lightbulb went off in Selig's head. He would buy the club and move it to Milwaukee!

According to Selig, he soon had a handshake agreement with Arthur Allyn to buy the White Sox and move them north. The American League was not keen on losing the city of Chicago as a base for one of its clubs, however, and blocked the sale.

Instead, Arthur Allyn sold his shares to his brother, John, and the team remained in the Windy City. Again, Selig's attempts to bring the big leagues back to Milwaukee had been thwarted.

"I figured that was our last chance," recalled Selig. "There was nowhere else to go. I can't tell you how disappointed I was. We had tried everything."

Well, not quite everything. Having been rebuffed in its attempts to land an expansion franchise, Selig's group turned their collective gaze to the Northwest, where the fledgling Seattle Pilots were in big trouble. Drawing only 677,944 fans in the club's inaugural 1969 season in Sick's Stadium, an expanded yet very minor league facility, owners Dewey and Max Soriano were losing their shirts.

The plan from the beginning was to build a new, domed ballpark for the Pilots, but the blueprints were never drawn up. The box seats at Sick's Stadium, which sold for a pricey $10, were actually folding metal chairs.

"It was a terrible ballpark," said Hegan. "I think there were four restrooms in the entire place. When you took a shower in the home clubhouse and somebody flushed a toilet in the bathroom next door, the water went cold."

The Sorianos received operating capital from investor William R. Daley, a former owner of the Cleveland Indians, but he didn't anticipate the club's expanding financial woes and eventually backed off. There were a few fruitless attempts to find local investors. Local theatre chain owner Fred Danz was ready to ride to the rescue until a local bank demanded payment of a previous $4 million loan, convincing him to step aside.

Hegan was so certain a local buyer would be found that he purchased a house in Seattle before he left for spring training.

"That's how much I thought we were going to stay," said Hegan. "It turned out to be a big mistake. I never lived in that house. It took me two years to sell it."

Smelling blood, the Milwaukee group swooped in and began secretly negotiating a deal to buy the Pilots. During Game 1 of the 1969 World Series, a handshake deal was made in which Selig and his investors would buy the club for $10.8 million and move it to Milwaukee.

Lamar Hunt and a group from Texas also showed interest in buying the Pilots, but the Milwaukee contingent got there first and made its preemptive strike. American League officials, who weren't keen on abandoning the Northwest after only one season, vowed to keep the team in Seattle and scheduled a meeting in March 1970 to vote on the matter.

In the meantime, the state of Washington filed an injunction to prevent the Pilots from moving. Team ownership responded by filing for bankruptcy, turning the matter over to the courts. That way, the Sorianos and league officials could wash their hands of the sticky situation, allowing Judge Volinn to make the decision for them.

Volinn did exactly that, ruling the team indeed was bankrupt and therefore would be sold to Selig's group for the agreed-upon price. Selig actually got the word late on March 31 that the ruling would go their way the next day. He was too excited to sleep.

The Seattle Pilots were dead. Long live the Milwaukee Brewers!

By the NUMBERS **30**—Brewers second baseman Tommy Harper became the first American League player to hit more than 30 home runs and steal more than 30 bases during the same season, with 31 and 38, respectively, in 1970.

If You Build It

Unlike the expansion Seattle Pilots, who played in a glorified minor league ballpark by the name of Sick's Stadium, the relocated Brewers had a suitable facility to call home. County Stadium had previously played host for 13 years to the Milwaukee Braves, who moved to Atlanta after the '65 season.

Showing remarkable foresight, the city's civic leaders pushed through plans in 1950 to build the stadium strictly on speculation, with hopes of drawing a major league franchise. The thinking was this: You're not a big-league city simply because you have a ballpark, but you have no chance without one. With no expansion planned for the major leagues, it took guts to go forward with a project that made many people nervous.

A teenager named Bud Selig, who 20 years later would bring a second major league club to town, remembered standing high atop Story Parkway and looking down upon the construction site. He was in high school at the time and already an avid baseball fan, thanks in large part to his mother's passion for the game.

"I couldn't believe we were going to have a double-deck ballpark in Milwaukee, a major-league stadium," said Selig, who often would stand in the freezing cold to watch construction workers flitting around like bees.

The first phase of construction was completed in March 1953, at a cost of some $6 million. In the ultimate example of the high-risk/high-reward business philosophy, the announcement came a mere two weeks later that the Boston Braves were coming to Milwaukee.

Tired of playing second fiddle to the favored Red Sox, Boston Braves owner Lou Perini figured it was time to seek greener pastures.

County Stadium on July 11, 1955. At that time the stadium had a capacity of 43,110. Photo courtesy of AP/Wide World Photos.

On March 13, he announced his intention to move the club to Milwaukee, and National League owners gave their stamp of approval five days later. Brand-new County Stadium had its first tenant.

And not just any tenant. In 13 seasons in Milwaukee, the Braves never had a losing season—the only professional sports franchise that can make that claim over that period of time. They shoved the demeaning "Bushville" label down the throats of the New York Yankees and their fans in the 1957 World Series and came within a whisker of doing likewise the following season.

Shortstop Johnny Logan, who played minor league baseball in Milwaukee before returning as a member of the 1953 Braves, was stunned at the transformation that took place among the city's fandom.

"Before the Braves came here, everybody in town was a Chicago Cubs fan," said Logan, who would continue to make his home in

TOP 10

Brewers Single-Season Home-Run Leaders

	Name	Year	Total
1.	Prince Fielder	2007	50
2.	Richie Sexson	2001	45
	Richie Sexson	2003	45
	Gorman Thomas	1979	45
5.	Ben Oglivie	1980	41
6.	Gorman Thomas	1982	39
7.	Jeromy Burnitz	1998	38
	Gorman Thomas	1980	38
9.	George Scott	1975	36
10.	Bill Hall	2006	35

Milwaukee after the Braves left for Atlanta. "That changed very quickly. I'll never forget our first Opening Day. It was cold but we still had 36,000 people in the stands (actually, 34,357). County Stadium became the place to be. The fan enthusiasm was great."

In terms of architectural design, County Stadium was no beauty queen, with its drab, gray color and corrugated metal exterior. But that didn't matter. Its prominent place in the growth of post–World War II Milwaukee could not be denied.

"Here was a community, after the war, searching for an identity," recalled Selig. "The Arena was built and the library, the museum, and the war memorial. And County Stadium became part of that growth. There were a lot of critics, not only of getting the stadium built but of where they were building it. That sounds familiar, doesn't it? Stadium controversies are a certainty of life, just like death and taxes."

Before Perini made his fateful decision to move the Braves, the city was prepared to move the minor league Brewers from old Borchert Field to County Stadium for its inaugural season. Instead, with big-league ball coming, local baseball fans were energized, and the team received a rousing parade through downtown upon its arrival at the train station. With some 60,000 admirers crowding the sidewalks, Braves manager Charlie Grimm proclaimed it "the great-est reception any ball club received from any town."

Though plans were quickly drawn to expand County Stadium beyond its original capacity, it became almost impossible to find good tickets. After drawing a measly 281,278 fans in their final season in Boston, the Braves surpassed the 1.8 million mark in their first season in Milwaukee, establishing a National League record.

In what baseball officials dubbed the "Milwaukee Miracle," the Braves attracted more than 2 million fans to County Stadium in each of the next four seasons. It was a rousing success story, especially considering the size of the town, and before long the Green Bay Packers decided to get in on the act and play part of their home schedule at the stadium, a two-hour drive to the south from storied Lambeau Field, then known as City Stadium.

"I really believe County Stadium helped save the Packers because they needed (financial) help back then," said Selig. "Drawing fans in Milwaukee was big for them."

The ballplayers never had it so good. They were second-class cit-izens in Boston, but in Milwaukee they were treated like kings. Restaurant meals were on the house, local car dealerships offered "loaners," meat factories and dairies showered them with free steaks, cheese, and milk. And let's not forget the beer. The local breweries climbed over each other to have their products associated with the players, who found cases stacked on their doorsteps.

Tom Kaminski, who served as a batboy when the Braves first arrived and later became an airline representative for the club, was constantly amazed at how Milwaukee fans fawned over the players. The attraction crossed all demographic boundaries, from factory workers to the city's rich and famous who traveled to the stadium from their lakeshore mansions.

DID YOU KNOW . . . In late June of 1970, 69-year-old Milt Mason, the first self-described "Bernie Brewer," camped out in a trailer atop the County Stadium scoreboard, vowing not to come down until the team drew a crowd of 40,000. The Brewers finally reached that figure on August 16.

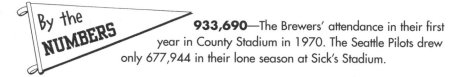

933,690—The Brewers' attendance in their first year in County Stadium in 1970. The Seattle Pilots drew only 677,944 in their lone season at Sick's Stadium.

"Everybody bent over backward for the team," said Kaminski. "County Stadium was nice and accessible, very convenient. People just wanted to be there."

Which made the Braves' rapid fall from grace all the more shocking. In 1958, despite repeating as National League champion, the club failed to draw 2 million fans to County Stadium for the first time in five years. Attendance continued to drop, which many blamed on a county board ruling in 1961 that prohibited carrying in beer. When the turnstiles clicked less than 800,000 times in '62, Perini decided to sell the club to a group of Chicago businessmen led by Bill Bartholomay.

It was the beginning of the end for the Milwaukee Braves. By late 1963, rumors of a move to Atlanta began to circulate. It was a stunning development that left the baseball-crazy Selig flabbergasted. He quickly formed a group called Teams, Inc., in an attempt to keep the Braves in town, but all legal attempts failed. After the lame-duck season of 1965, during which the team drew only 555,584 fans, the Braves relocated to Atlanta.

Other than the few Packers games played there, County Stadium stood mostly dark for the next four years. Selig's group worked feverishly to bring Major League Baseball back to the city, but those efforts were thwarted time after time. It took a bankruptcy proceeding in Seattle in early 1970 for Milwaukee to get another team, the reborn Brewers. With that unexpected turn of events, the stadium came alive again.

The old ballpark served the Brewers well for many years, but it became apparent to Selig and his ownership group in the late '80s that County Stadium was on the endangered species list. Baseball economics took a turn for the

TRIVIA

Which team did Milwaukee Braves ace Warren Spahn beat for his 300th career victory on August 11, 1961, at County Stadium?

Answers to the trivia questions are on page 147.

worse, and Selig began floating the notion that his club could not survive without a new facility.

That grim reality hit hard in cities across the country, but the battle in Milwaukee over financing a new ballpark was as fierce as any, if not more so. Nearly 10 years passed from the original debates until ground was broken for Miller Park in November 1996.

A tragic crane collapse in July 1999 killed three ironworkers, delayed construction of the new facility, and added one year to the life of County Stadium. There was a rousing sendoff at the end of the 2000 season, with many of the old Braves and Brewers who had played there returning for a fond farewell. It was time for the old gray lady to go, but that didn't stop longtime fans from shedding tears when demolition crews starting swinging the wrecking ball.

TRIVIA

What two years was the All-Star Game played at County Stadium?

Answers to the trivia questions are on page 147.

"County Stadium produced, for two to three generations of people, great memories," said Selig. "It was a bond between fathers, mothers, and children. You can ask yourself, 'Because of County Stadium, was Milwaukee and Wisconsin a better place to live?' The answer is so clearly yes that it's not even worth debate."

The Kid

To put it kindly, the Brewers of the early years were a bit challenged. They lost 97 games in their inaugural season in 1970, followed by campaigns of 92 and 91 losses. Three years into their existence, they were a whopping 81 games below .500 in overall play.

Thus, when a gangly 18-year-old shortstop by the name of Robin Yount showed up in Sun City, Arizona, in the spring of 1974, with all of 64 games of minor league experience under his belt, manager Del Crandall began asking his staff if there was any good reason he shouldn't make the team. Other than the fact that he was a teenager, incredibly raw, and about to be asked to play one of the most important positions in the field.

It wasn't as if the Brewers would have to punt an All-Star off the position. The previous season, Tim Johnson batted an underwhelming .213 while committing 25 errors at short. Why not give the kid a chance, indeed?

"The Kid." It was a nickname immediately hung on Yount for obvious reasons. As often is the case with such monikers, it stuck with him for his entire 20-year career with the Brewers, long after "The Kid" had evolved into a grizzled veteran with his youth far in the rearview mirror.

For the life of him, Yount can't remember who first called him "The Kid."

"When you're 18, you're 'The Kid,'" he said. "What else are they going to call you? I'm sure they all called me that. It was better than some other things they could have called me."

One day, near the end of spring training, Yount filed onto the team bus for a short trip across town for an exhibition game.

Suddenly, he was summoned to the front, where Crandall was in the manager's traditional first seat. Yount was trembling as he made it up the aisle. "I figured he was either going to tell me I made the team or that I was going down [to the minors]," recalled Yount. "I wasn't sure which one it was going to be. It wouldn't have been a shock to be sent out."

Happily for Yount, and for the franchise, the news was good. Yount would be the Brewers' Opening Day shortstop. His Hall of Fame career was about to begin, improbably, unpredictably, seemingly out of nowhere.

All rookies need a mentor to help guide the way, and Yount found one almost immediately in hitting Coach Harvey Kuenn, a former big-league batting star. Kuenn immediately saw something he liked in Yount and took him under his wing, shielding him from those who wanted to offer unsolicited advice.

"I remember the first time they brought Robin to spring training," recalled Bob Uecker, the Brewers' Hall of Fame radio broadcaster. "Harvey was one of the guys who said, 'Don't mess with him.' Harvey was a batting champion and a great hitter. Robin was somewhat unorthodox but Harvey knew it was whatever gets it done for you. He probably saw a lot of himself in Robin."

Kuenn saw that Yount already had the proper approach to the game, a no-nonsense, grind-it-out mentality that helped him overcome mistakes. And, in the early going, there were plenty of mistakes. Yount committed only 19 errors in 107 games his rookie year (he missed the last month or so with a bad ankle), but that total ballooned to an eye popping 44 in his sophomore season.

"That was a tough year," said Yount. "A fielding slump is like a hitting slump. You lose your confidence and the whole nine yards. It gets into your head after a while. You just get back on the horse. I'd get back on and fall off again. It was basically on-the-job training. My second year was by far the most difficult year of my career. It took me a number of years before I really felt like I was a major league player."

It was a trial by fire that would have broken mentally weak players, but it only made Yount more determined to improve. Crandall, Kuenn, and the rest of the coaching staff soon discovered that work ethic would not be a problem with this youngster. And that never changed over the 20 years Yount played for the Brewers. He knew how to play the game only one way—full-steam ahead, pedal to the metal.

Yount credits his older brother, Larry, for instilling that work ethic in him. Larry Yount was a promising pitcher whose career with the Houston Astros was cut short before he ever faced a batter in the major leagues. He was warming for his first appearance and injured his arm, which goes beyond having tough luck. But Larry Yount gave his younger brother some advice that he never forgot.

TRIVIA

Which pitcher surrendered Robin Yount's 3,000ᵗʰ career hit on September 9, 1992?

Answers to the trivia questions are on page 147.

"He used to preach that you're only going to be on the field for three hours, so while you're out there, give it everything you've got," Yount recalled. "He said, 'If you want to relax and take it easy or something, you can do that on your own time. But when you're out there, give it everything you've got.' When you're young, you don't want to listen to your brother telling you stuff like that, but it was true."

That lesson would help Yount become the epitome of the professional ballplayer. For 20 years, no one questioned his unwavering dedication to the game. If he hit a sharp comebacker to the pitcher, he dropped his bat, lowered his head, and ran hard to first. For all of the young players who followed him to the big leagues with the Brewers, Yount became the ultimate example of how to play the game the right way.

The way Yount saw it, part of his job description meant playing while he was hurt. Unlike today's game, where some players will miss a week with a hangnail, it almost took an act of Congress to get Yount out of the lineup. If he could walk, even with a limp, he figured he could play.

John Adam, the trainer during much of Yount's stay in Milwaukee, lost many a verbal battle over the wisdom of being on the field at certain times.

"He woke up each day thinking that he was going to play a baseball game and, really, nothing was going to stop that," Adam said.

"That was his sole focus, that he had a game to play that day. He would foul balls off his lower leg and from his knee to his ankle it would be solid purple and full of fluid. But there was never a doubt he was going to play."

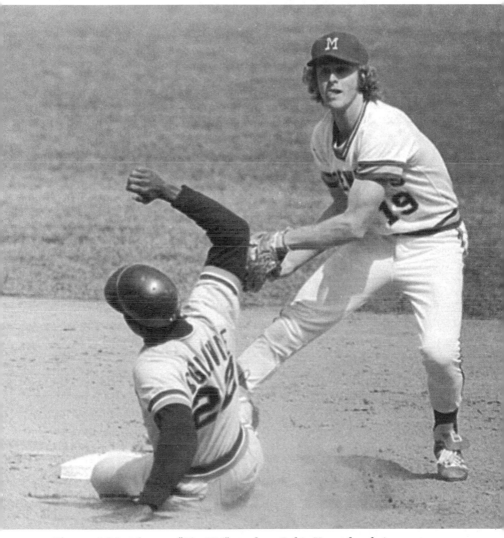

The youthful nickname "The Kid" stuck on Robin Yount for obvious reasons when he first arrived in Milwaukee, but he quickly demonstrated superstar talent by playing with a skill beyond his years. Photo courtesy of Getty Images.

By the NUMBERS **3,142**—Career hits for Robin Yount, which ranks 17ᵗʰ on the all-time list.

Yount still holds the club record of 276 consecutive games played. That streak ended on June 14, 1989, with what officially were called "badly bruised knees." In reality, Yount's knees were a wreck. The team doctor drained both on several occasions, allowing Yount to stay on the field. Many a player would have shut it down long before then, but Yount pressed on, barely able to walk but still figuring he could help in some way.

"More often than not, if things were bothering me, I felt I could play through them," Yount said. "Guys are hurting all the time. That goes with the game. But there are things that hurt that you can play with.

"I ended up having arguments once in a while, but that's okay. The manager didn't feel like I could play, and that's his job. That doesn't mean I'm going to like his decision all the time. He may not have liked the way I was looking, and he was probably right. But in my heart I felt like I could play."

One injury Yount couldn't shake off occurred in 1984, dramatically changing the course of his career. Over his first 10 years in the majors, Yount established himself as one of the top shortstops in the game. He won the American League Most Valuable Player Award in 1982, leading the Brewers to the World Series with a tremendous offensive season, batting .331 with 29 home runs and 114 runs batted in.

But by the end of the '84 season, Yount could barely get the ball over to first base. His shoulder finally broke down under the wear and tear of playing the most demanding position on the field, forcing Yount to undergo surgery. When Yount still had no zip on his throws the following spring, the decision was made to move him to the outfield. At first, he went to left field, but by the middle of the season was in center field to stay. Yet another shoulder surgery was necessary that September, guaranteeing Yount would never return to the infield.

"That was really frustrating," Yount recalled. "That really took away some of my ability, my God-given ability, because I had a pretty good throwing arm. After that happened, I never had a good throwing arm again. I didn't want to go to the outfield. I was thinking that it would be temporary and that my arm would come back and I'd go back to short."

To the surprise of no one who knew Yount, he soon embraced his new position and became more than adequate in center. Still a graceful runner with long, ground-swallowing strides, he excelled at patrolling the outfield gaps, making up for what he lacked in true speed with his natural baseball instincts.

Yount utilized those instincts to provide a dramatic, spine-tingling finish to one of the greatest games in franchise history on April 15, 1987, in Baltimore's Memorial Stadium. With young lefty Juan Nieves one out away from pitching the first no-hitter in franchise history, Orioles first baseman Eddie Murray sent a drive to right-center that had extra-base hit written all over it. Yount refused to read that handwriting, however, racing over and making a sensational diving catch, fully stretched out as he cradled the ball in his glove.

"That catch by Robin was incredible," said Nieves, whose no-hitter highlighted the Brewers' record 13–0 start. "I'll never forget that as long as I live."

Some players forced from their original positions by injuries are never heard from again. But Yount continued to prosper. In 1989, seven years after winning his first MVP award, Yount repeated the feat, this time as a 33 year old center fielder. He became only the third player to claim MVP honors at different positions, joining the select company of Hall of Famers Stan Musial and Hank Greenberg.

On September 9, 1992, at County Stadium, Yount punched his ticket to Cooperstown by collecting the 3,000th hit of his career

DID YOU KNOW . . . Robin Yount is one of five players in Brewers history to hit for the cycle, accomplishing the feat on June 12, 1988, at Chicago. The others are Mike Hegan (September 3, 1976, at Detroit), Charlie Moore (October 1, 1980, at California), Paul Molitor (May 15, 1991, at Minnesota), and Chad Moeller (April 27, 2004, vs. Cincinnati).

TOP 10

Highest Batting Averages in Club History

	Name	Year	Average
1.	Paul Molitor	1987	.353
2.	Cecil Cooper	1980	.352
3.	Robin Yount	1982	.331
	David Nilsson	1996	.331
5.	Willie Randolph	1991	.327
6.	Jeff Cirillo	1999	.326
7.	Paul Molitor	1991	.325
	Jeff Cirillo	1996	.325
9.	Ryan Braun	2007	.324
10.	Paul Molitor	1979	.322

against Cleveland's Jose Mesa. He was the third-youngest player to reach that plateau, trailing only Ty Cobb and Hank Aaron.

Yount's productivity declined in subsequent years, but he continued to find ways to contribute. In the process, a new generation of players learned to play the game properly by watching his daily example.

"He knew he wasn't the most athletic guy in baseball, so in order to get ahead he had to work hard," said Larry Yount. "He seldom beat himself. Instead, he figured out ways to win. Being able to stay focused was his greatest asset. He always stayed one step ahead of them. He came to play."

"The Kid" knew no other way.

If I Had a Hammer

After the Brewers suffered through their fifth consecutive losing season in 1974, team president Bud Selig was looking for something to give his franchise a "shot in the arm." The Brewers had surpassed the 1 million mark in attendance in 1973, only to dip below that level in '74.

Selig's father was a longtime car dealer in Milwaukee and taught his son the value of promotional gimmicks to spur sales. Applying that tactic to his baseball club, Selig came up with a brilliant plan: Bring Hank Aaron back to Milwaukee.

Aaron began his Hall of Fame career with the Milwaukee Braves in 1954 after playing minor league ball in tiny Eau Claire, Wisconsin, in the western part of the state. "I always considered Wisconsin and Milwaukee my second home," said Aaron. "That's where it all began for me."

Selig, who had forged a close relationship with Aaron, figured the home-run king might be receptive to leaving Atlanta and returning to his roots in Milwaukee. The 40-year-old Aaron had gone through the fishbowl atmosphere of breaking Babe Ruth's record in the first month of the '74 season, with the intense pressure, racist threats, and media spotlight a bit much for a quiet, introspective man from Mobile, Alabama.

During the 1974 World Series, Selig traveled to Atlanta and met with Aaron and Bill Bartholomay, chairman of the Braves. It was Bartholomay who broke Selig's heart by moving the Braves from Milwaukee after the 1965 season, but the two later became friends and let bygones be bygones. The talks continued over several days, with Selig later meeting with Bartholomay between Milwaukee and Chicago, where Bartholomay had a home.

Finally, on November 2, a deal was struck. The Brewers sent out-fielder Dave May and a player to be named (minor league pitcher Roger Alexander) to Atlanta for Aaron. Selig could not contain his excitement upon announcing the trade.

"It was stunning, really," said Selig. "It was great for the city of Milwaukee and the fans. Getting Hank to come back and wear a Brewers uniform was remarkable. Nobody expected anything like that. And Hank was excited about it, too. It was like coming home for him. It was really, really big."

So big that 48,160 fans flocked to County Stadium on a frigid, 37-degree afternoon for "Welcome Home, Henry Day" on April 11. With Aaron in the number three spot in the lineup in his new role as designated hitter—something totally foreign to a National League born-and-bred player—the Brewers made the day a complete success with a 6–2 victory over Cleveland.

"It was a very emotional day, for me and Hank," recalled Selig. "Hank was really happy to be back. He couldn't believe the response from the fans. It was a very exciting day."

The other players could not believe they were sharing the same clubhouse with baseball's home-run king. Shortstop Robin Yount, a mere 19 and trying to find his way as a sophomore in the big leagues, couldn't believe his ears when he first heard that Aaron was returning to his Milwaukee roots.

"It was tough not to be in awe of him," said Yount. "I mean, this was the all-time home-run king. Obviously, he wasn't the same player he was earlier in his career, but he was still Hank Aaron.

"At first, I didn't know if I should go up and try to talk to him. He was a pretty quiet guy. But it wasn't like he stayed to himself. There were times he would come over and give you advice. He just wasn't a real outgoing guy. It was good for the organization and the city to have him on the team. I know it was a pretty big deal to me. I think he welcomed it and Milwaukee certainly welcomed him

Henry "Hank" Aaron holds up his new uniform along with Milwaukee Brewers Manager Del Crandall in 1974 after Aaron signed a contract to play with the Brewers as a designated hitter. Photo courtesy of Bettman/CORBIS.

back. He wanted to end his career where he started, so it made a lot of sense."

It was obvious that Aaron's best days were behind him. Despite getting to rest his 41-year-old legs by serving as the DH, he batted only .234 that season with 12 home runs and 60 RBIs. But no one expected him to terrorize the league. His mere presence gave a sense of legitimacy to a fledgling franchise desperate to become relevant. And his return had the desired effect at the gate, as the Brewers set a club record by drawing more than 1.2 million fans to County Stadium.

Aaron's skills further deteriorated in 1976, prompting him to announce his retirement, effective at the end of the season. His body finally giving out on him, Aaron played little after the All-Star break. Jim Gantner, a young infielder summoned from the minors when Don Money was injured, often found himself sitting next to Aaron on the bench during games. And, much to Gantner's amazement, Aaron willingly engaged him in discussions about hitting. For a young player just beginning his major league journey, it was a heady experience.

"When I was a kid, I'd throw the ball against the garage, pretending I was Hank Aaron or Eddie Mathews," said Gantner, a Wisconsin native from the tiny town of Eden. "Now, here I was playing with him. He was the DH, so he'd be on the bench when we were in the field. If I wasn't playing, I'd try to sit next to him and talk about hitting.

TRIVIA

Which pitcher surrendered the final hit of Hank Aaron's career?

Answers to the trivia questions are on page 147.

"I asked him, 'What do you look for on the first pitch?' Things like that. He'd tell me what the pitchers were trying to do. They were pitching him inside a lot because he was older and they didn't think he'd get around on the ball. He'd say, 'I have to cheat a little bit now when they come inside.' He knew what they were trying to do to him. Just sitting there, talking hitting with Hank Aaron, it didn't get any better than that."

When the Brewers took the field on July 20 to play the California Angels, it was just another nondescript day of a long season. There

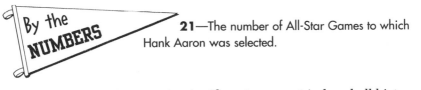

was no reason to expect a significant moment in baseball history as two last-place clubs met with a scant 10,134 fans in the stands at County Stadium.

Angels reliever Dick Drago was working in his fourth inning and starting to tire when George "Boomer" Scott hammered a two-run homer, bringing Aaron to the plate. Drago had retired Aaron on a fastball in his previous at-bat but this time opted to start with a slider. He hung it and Aaron turned on it, knocking it over the left-field fence.

"I remember being upset because I had gotten him out (earlier in the game) with fastballs," recalled Drago, who surrendered only seven homers in 79 innings that season. "I was a fastball pitcher and I out-thought myself.

"The thing about hitters, the last thing to go is their bat speed. Their legs go, their arms go, but they can still swing the bat. That's why you see old-timers in 'legends' games and they can still swing the bat. A guy like [Aaron] is always considered dangerous until the end of his career.

"It wasn't really important at the time. Now, I'm an answer in *Trivial Pursuit*. 'Who gave up Hank Aaron's last home run?'"

It was the 10th homer of Aaron's season and the 755th of his career. There was no way to know at the time it would be Aaron's last homer, not with 76 games remaining on the Brewers' schedule. But he played sparingly down the stretch, logging only 61 more at-bats as manager Alex Grammas began looking at younger players.

Number 755 would be the benchmark for all sluggers to follow in Aaron's path. (Aaron's record was finally eclipsed, by San Francisco's Barry Bonds, in 2007.)

Aaron remembers little about the homer, other than the fact that he never got the ball back. As it rattled around beyond the left-field fence, Richard Arndt, a member of the grounds crew, dashed over and retrieved it. Arndt supposedly offered to return the ball to Aaron after the game on one condition: that he be allowed to meet the home-run king and hand the ball over in person.

TOP 10

Most Career Strikeouts in Club History

	Name	Strikeouts
1.	Robin Yount	1,350
2.	Geoff Jenkins	1,118
3.	Gorman Thomas	1,033
4.	Paul Molitor	882
5.	Rob Deer	823
6.	Greg Vaughn	761
7.	Cecil Cooper	721
8.	Jeromy Burnitz	680
9.	Jose Valentin	585
10.	Don Money	539

Not only was that request denied, but Arndt was fired the next day for refusing to surrender the baseball. As the story goes, Arndt was even docked $5 from his final paycheck to cover the cost of the ball.

"They said I'd been terminated for taking Brewers property," Arndt said.

Aaron later wrote in his autobiography that he offered $10,000 to Arndt for the ball, but he wouldn't sell it. Arndt moved to Albuquerque, New Mexico, and took the ball with him.

"To me, that ball is just as important as the one from number 715, because it's the one that established the record," Aaron wrote. "The record is 755, not 715."

Several years later, Arndt pulled a fast one over on Aaron, taking the ball to an autograph show in Phoenix at which Aaron was appearing. Without realizing the significance of the ball he held in his hands, Aaron autographed it and handed it back to Arndt.

Arndt eventually sold the ball for $650,000 to an undisclosed buyer believed to be Andrew J. Knuth of Westport, Connecticut. To his credit, Arndt donated $155,800 (25 percent) from the sale to Aaron's charitable Chasing the Dream Foundation, Inc., established to help underprivileged children develop their artistic talents. But

Aaron believes the ball belongs in the National Baseball Hall of Fame in Cooperstown, New York.

"If I had the ball, that's what I would have done with it," said Aaron. "I tried getting it from that kid."

Aaron suited up as a major leaguer for the final time on October 3. Despite his declining physical condition, he managed to leg out an infield single in the sixth inning, driving in the 2,297[th] run of his career. In the Brewers' dugout, Grammas turned to Gantner, the raw, rookie infielder, and said, "Get in there. You're pinch-running for 'Hammer.'"

"I said, 'You're kidding me,'" recalled Gantner. "I knew it was going to be history. Hank shook my hand as I came in and went off the field. Here I am, on first base, pinch-running for one of my idols in his last at-bat in the big leagues. It's right there in the record books."

Aaron trotted off to a standing ovation from the County Stadium crowd. His Hall of Fame career was over.

Bambi's Bombers

It was the first day of spring training in 1978. Gorman Thomas was walking through the Brewers clubhouse with a cup of coffee in his hand when he encountered a squatty, balding old man he had never seen before.

"Who the [bleep] are you?" snarled the power-hitting center fielder.

"Who the f*ck are you?" the stranger replied feistily.

"It doesn't matter. I'm a player," said Thomas.

"Well, it does matter because I'm George Bamberger," said the stranger.

"Oh, hi, George," said Thomas, trying his best to hide his embarrassment.

Totally unfazed by the rude welcome, Bamberger told Thomas, "You're my starting center fielder. The job is yours. Don't lose it."

And that's how Thomas was introduced to the Brewers' new manager. After two 95-loss seasons under Alex Grammas, general manager Harry Dalton decided the Brewers needed a change in direction. He chose Bamberger, who had no managerial experience yet but was a highly successful pitching coach with the Baltimore Orioles, working for legendary manager Earl Weaver.

Bamberger was a native of Staten Island, New York, but Dalton figured he'd be a perfect fit in the blue-collar surroundings of the Midwest. Bamberger cussed like a sailor at times, didn't mind having a beer or two at local taverns, loved to fish, and exuded an every-man persona that quickly endeared him to Milwaukeeans.

The players quickly grew to love the straight-talking Bamberger as well. After their initial "who the heck are you?" encounter,

Gorman Thomas was the Seattle Pilots' first and only first-round draft pick in June 1969 as a shortstop/right-handed pitcher out of James Island High School in Charleston, South Carolina.

Thomas and Bamberger grew very close. It was easy to see why. In essence, Thomas was a younger version of his manager, a gruff, profane, beer-loving yet hard-playing slugger who came to epitomize the blue-collar nature of the team's fandom.

"Without George Bamberger, I would not have had a career," Thomas said without hesitation.

Though Bamberger was known for developing 20-game winners in Baltimore—he had four in 1971 in Jim Palmer, Mike Cuellar, Dave McNally, and Pat Dobson—he was a devout advocate of Weaver's "School of the Three-Run Homer." Bamberger loved bombing opponents into submission, one of the reasons he was so fond of the home-run hitting Thomas.

On Opening Day, Bamberger put Thomas in the starting lineup in center field. The Brewers beat Bamberger's former team, the Orioles, but no thanks to the free-swinging Thomas, who whiffed four times. Afterward, Bamberger strolled over to Thomas's locker and put his hand on the player's shoulder.

"He said, 'Hey, you big so-and-so. I didn't need you today. Maybe you'll give me something tomorrow,'" recalled Thomas.

The next day, "Stormin' Gorman" socked a grand slam.

Bamberger inherited a team ready to take off. Joining Thomas in a power-packed lineup were the likes of Cecil Cooper, Larry Hisle, Sixto Lezcano, Don Money, Sal Bando, and a rookie by the name of Paul Molitor filling in for the injured Robin Yount at shortstop.

As the Brewers continued to sock balls into the stratosphere, they soon became known as "Bambi's Bombers," one of those great nicknames that fit like a well-worn batting glove. After nine seasons of losing, the Brewers started to win under Bamberger, a player's manager who made out the lineup card and basically stayed out of the way.

The Brewers won 93 games in '78, finishing in third place in the tough AL East, only six and a half games off the pace set by the mighty

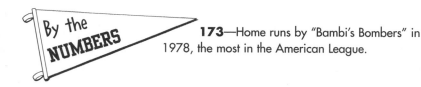

173—Home runs by "Bambi's Bombers" in 1978, the most in the American League.

New York Yankees. Milwaukee fans embraced the club, putting 1.6 million fannies in the seats of County Stadium, an increase of nearly a half-million from the previous season. For his efforts, Bamberger was named American League Manager of the Year.

The winning continued in 1979. Now a legitimate contender, the Brewers finished with a 95–66 record, good for second place behind the Orioles, as Thomas led the league with 45 homers. Better yet, the club drew 1,918,343 fans to County Stadium, by far the largest attendance in club history.

"The reason we won is George gave people a chance to play," said Thomas. "The impetus wasn't put on you to have a monster game. He let you play, even if you failed for a while. I got a chance to play every day. I hit ninth but that's a hell of a lot better than batting 10th. He was the greatest guy."

Bamberger's own professional career began in 1946 and included a short major league stint. He pitched for the New York Giants and Baltimore Orioles, going 0–0 in 10 major league games. In 1963, he retired as a player-coach in the minors and became the Orioles' minor league pitching coordinator. Five years later, he was named the Orioles' pitching coach.

Bamberger was not a manager who benched a player mired in a hitting slump. Toward the end of the '78 season, Thomas was stuck on 31 home runs for several days, becoming increasingly frustrated. But Bambi stuck with his all-or-nothing slugger.

"Thirty-one was George's number," said Thomas. "One day I said, 'Damn it, George. Why couldn't you have No. 64?'"

One thing the Brewers learned to do under Bamberger was beat the hated Yankees. With mouthy manager Billy Martin, pompous slugger Reggie Jackson, and free-spending owner George Steinbrenner, New York was the evil empire, as far as Milwaukee fans were concerned. And the Brewers became a thorn in the side of the Yankees, going 35–25 against them from 1978 through their World Series year of 1982.

One of the Brewers' most memorable victories over the Yankees came on July 27, 1979, at County Stadium. In a back-and-forth game that had 47,929 fans howling throughout the night, Cooper socked three home runs, including the game-winner in the bottom of the ninth off flame-throwing reliever Goose Gossage. That game was spiced by a bench-clearing brawl in the fourth inning, started by a confrontation between Brewers lefty Mike Caldwell and Jackson.

"It's one of the greatest memories that I had as a player," Cooper said of that electric evening.

Shortly before the start of his third season with the Brewers in 1980, Bamberger suffered a heart attack in Arizona. He underwent bypass surgery and was forced to hand the managerial reins to Buck Rodgers until June. Bambi did not lose his well-honed sense of humor, however, nor his loyalty to his adoring fans. Recuperating at his Florida home, he taped a video message that was shown on the scoreboard at County Stadium on Opening Day.

"I'd like to thank the fans," said Bamberger. "I'd like to wish the ballplayers much success. We've got very capable coaches who know their business."

And then, in a classic Bambi moment, he finished by saying, "So, sit back, enjoy the game and have a beer on me."

After a testy first meeting, Gorman Thomas and the rest of the Brewers warmed up to new manager George Bamberger, shown here in 1978. Photo courtesy of Getty Images.

TOP 10

Most Games Started for the Brewers During a Pitcher's Career

	Name	Games Started
1.	Jim Slaton	268
2.	Moose Haas	231
3.	Mike Caldwell	217
4.	Bill Wegman	216
5.	Teddy Higuera	205
6.	Ben Sheets	190
7.	Cal Eldred	169
8.	Chris Bosio	163
9.	Bill Travers	157
10.	Jaime Navarro	156

A roar went up among the sellout crowd, followed by the loud chants, "Bambi! Bambi! Bambi!"

That day was known more for the performance of Lezcano, who socked two home runs, including a game-winning, ninth-inning grand slam against the Boston Red Sox. In the middle of the game, Dalton decided to have some fun with his absent manager. He placed a call to Bamberger, told him the score, and said, "By the way, you owe us $57,000."

"Why?" asked Bambi.

"Because everybody is having a beer on you. They're all signing your name to the tab," Dalton said with a big laugh.

Lezcano hit his dramatic grand slam in the bottom of the ninth off Boston reliever Dick Drago, who four years earlier surrendered Hank Aaron's 755th and final home run at County Stadium while pitching for the California Angels. Afterward, amid a raucous clubhouse celebration, Lezcano lifted a can of beer and said, "This is for Bambi."

Even in their beloved manager's absence, "Bambi's Bombers" continued to pound opponents into submission, with Thomas, Cooper, and Ben Oglivie all knocking in more than 100 runs that season. But the Brewers took a step backwards, winning only 86 games and finishing third. In September, Bamberger announced he was stepping down as manager. He got the managing itch again in 1982 and agreed to manage the New York Mets that season. But Bambi later admitted he missed Milwaukee.

"It's a city that's one of a kind," he said at the time.

Dalton gave the prodigal manager a chance to return by re-hiring him as manager before the 1985 season. Bamberger would lead the Brewers until September 1986, when he retired with nine games remaining in the season. This time, Bambi was done as a manager, but he firmly etched his name in franchise lore before retiring to Florida and his second passion, fishing.

TRIVIA

Who was the first Brewer to be voted to the starting lineup in the All-Star Game?

Answers to the trivia questions are on page 147.

"There was something about George," said Bud Selig, then-owner of the Brewers. "He was perfect for Milwaukee, a wonderful personality and a unique guy, just a wonderful human being."

Rollie Saves the Day

After the 1980 season, general manager Harry Dalton changed the course of the franchise by making a bold trade with the St. Louis Cardinals.

Seeking more of a veteran presence on his club, Dalton sent outfielders Sixto Lezcano and David Green and pitchers Lary Sorensen and Dave LaPoint to the Cardinals for All-star Catcher Ted Simmons, right-hander Pete Vuckovich, and reliever Rollie Fingers, at the time the all-time save leader in baseball.

Lezcano was something of a local hero in Milwaukee and Green was considered the organization's top prospect, but Dalton knew he had to give up something to acquire three players who played huge roles in getting the Brewers to the World Series in 1982.

How many managers pick up two future Cy Young Award winners in one trade? That's what Dalton did in acquiring Fingers, who claimed the award in 1981, and Vuckovich, the winner the following season.

The Cardinals, who had acquired Fingers from San Diego only four days previously at those same winter meetings, already had one of the top closers in the game in Bruce Sutter. Dalton knew St. Louis wouldn't keep both, and the two cagey general managers began a cat-and-mouse game. Dalton wanted Fingers, but Cardinals general manager Whitey Herzog insisted on getting the multitalented Green back in the deal.

"He was on the list of people we wouldn't trade," Dalton said of Green. "It got to the point where we had a deal on paper but they still wanted David Green. The last several hours, we were still saying no."

Dalton eventually said yes, but despite acquiring the three proven veterans, he didn't feel giddy afterward.

"I had a little buyer's remorse afterward," Dalton admitted. "I wondered if I had done the right thing."

It didn't take long for Dalton to stop second-guessing himself. During the strike-split 1981 season, Fingers put together one of the greatest seasons of any relief pitcher in big-league history. Relying primarily on a sharp-breaking slider, he led the majors with 28 saves, helping the Brewers advance to the American League playoffs for the first time.

When all was said and done, Fingers not only was the AL Cy Young Award winner, he was league MVP as well, a daily double that no relief pitcher had previously accomplished. On August 21, 1982, he would become the first reliever to notch 300 career saves.

Green, the key to the deal from the Cardinals' side, never realized his potential. Battling alcohol problems that sapped his natural athletic ability, he played in only 489 games in the majors before retiring, accumulating only 374 career hits.

The Brewers clinched the second-half championship on the penultimate day of the season with a 2–1 victory over Detroit. With

During the strike-split 1981 season, Rollie Fingers put together one of the greatest seasons of any relief pitcher in big-league history. Photo courtesy of Getty Images.

TRIVIA

What was manager "Buck" Rodgers's real name?

Answers to the trivia questions are on page 147.

Milwaukee leading Detroit by one game in the AL East, the Tigers sent ace Jack Morris to the mound and the Brewers countering with their big-game pitcher, Vuckovich. As might be expected, the game settled into a tense pitchers' duel.

The Brewers scored twice in the bottom of the eighth to erase a 1–0 deficit, then turned it over to Fingers, who had recorded the final out in the top of that inning. Fingers ended it by striking out Lou Whitaker, one of the most memorable moments in club history, touching off a mob scene at the mound.

"Rollie dominated that year," said second baseman Jim Gantner. "The key was getting him and Vuckie and Simba [Simmons] in that trade. They got us over the hump."

It got a bit wild afterward in the home clubhouse, with both Dalton and team owner Bud Selig getting dunked in the whirlpool. Selig's first request afterward was to get help in fishing out his eyeglasses. Amid a torrent of champagne spray, Vuckovich was quaffing his customary beer (or two or three).

"That's what it was all about," said Vuckovich, who certainly lived up to his part in Dalton's big trade by going 14–4 with a 3.55 ERA in 24 games. "You're all in it for that common goal: to win. When you win, all the tough times along the way were worth it."

The Brewers went on to push the powerful New York Yankees to the full five games before bowing out in the opening round of playoffs. That experience proved to be a springboard for the next season, when the Brewers made their first and only appearance in the World Series.

"You have to get over that first hurdle," said first baseman Cecil Cooper. "Then, you know you belong. You could see that growth process taking place. That night, we finally got over the hump."

DID YOU KNOW . . . Robin Yount became one of the youngest players in major league history to collect 1,000 hits at the age of 24 on August 16, 1980.

TOP 10

Brewers Career Saves Leaders

	Name	Saves
1.	Dan Plesac	133
2.	Rollie Fingers	97
3.	Mike Fetters	79
	Bob Wickman	79
5.	Derrick Turnbow	64
6.	Doug Henry	61
	Ken Sanders	61
	Dan Kolb	61
9.	Francisco Cordero	60
10.	Doug Jones	49

The following fall, the Brewers might have gotten over the biggest hump of all, the World Series, if not for an arm injury that sidelined Fingers in the postseason after he had compiled 29 saves. With Fingers unavailable to record the final outs, the Brewers lost in seven games to the Cardinals, who finished off the AL champs in Game 7 with Sutter, the closer Herzog kept.

To this day, everyone associated with that club insists the Brewers would have won the big ring had Fingers been available for duty.

"No question about it," said Cooper. "If we had Rollie, we would have won. They had their closer and we didn't have ours. It was a crushing blow. Rollie was 'The Man.'"

Fingers was elected to the National Baseball Hall of Fame in 1992, joining Hoyt Wilhelm at the time as the only two relief pitchers so honored. He was enshrined in Cooperstown representing the Oakland A's, the team for which he first experienced glory in the mid-'70s. The man with the handlebar moustache is a pioneer of modern relief pitching, helping define the role of closer for those who followed him.

But, unlike closers of the '90s and the new millennium, Fingers often pitched multiple innings. Workhorse relievers such as Fingers

By the NUMBERS **0**—The number of earned runs allowed by Rollie Fingers in converting his major league-high total of 28 saves in 1981.

and Gossage thought nothing of pitching two or three innings to finish games, if necessary. For instance, in his wonderful 1981 season, Fingers pitched 78 innings in only 47 appearances, yet still compiled a sparkling 1.04 ERA. With San Diego, Fingers led the NL with 35 saves in 1977 and 37 in 1978. Making a huge impact in the 1974 World Series with two saves and one victory, he was named MVP in the A's triumph over the Los Angeles Dodgers.

It was that kind of dependability that Dalton sought when he acquired Fingers from the Cardinals. Unfortunately, Fingers never was the same after suffering the arm injury late in the '82 season. He sat out the entire 1983 season and was only a shadow of his former self before being released by the Brewers in 1985.

But, during that breakthrough 1981 season and for most of that glorious campaign in 1982, Fingers was worth his weight in moustache wax. Even though he pitched for the Brewers for only five seasons, the club retired his No. 34 on August 9, 1992, in ceremonies at County Stadium.

"When Rollie came in from the bullpen, you pretty much knew the game was over," said second baseman Jim Gantner. "He was almost automatic. If we had the lead late in games, we knew we were going to win. I know we would have won the World Series if he would have been able to pitch."

Harvey's Wallbangers

It might have been the shortest clubhouse meeting ever held by a major league manager.

On June 2, 1982, the Brewers were in Seattle, preparing for the finale of a three-game series in Seattle, in the dark, dank, cavernous Kingdome. As the players began filtering into the visiting clubhouse, they heard the news that manager Buck Rodgers had been fired and replaced with longtime hitting coach Harvey Kuenn.

The players gathered for a pregame meeting with Kuenn, anxious to see what their new leader had to say.

"There's just two things I want you to know," said Kuenn. "Number one, I don't like meetings. Number two, this meeting is over. You guys go out and play."

End of meeting.

It was classic Harvey Kuenn. Succinct, matter-of-fact, no-nonsense. The man the players called "Arch" saw no need for a fiery Knute Rockne–style speech, no reason to try to motivate a group of veterans with gobs of talent. Just go out and play.

Switching managers really wasn't a difficult decision for general manager Harry Dalton. Despite the obvious talent on hand, the club foundered under the hands-on approach of manager Buck Rodgers, who guided the club to its first playoff berth in the strike-split '81 season. The Brewers were 23–24 on June 2, tied for fifth place in the competitive AL East, seven games out of first. Dalton wisely opted for a man the players loved and respected.

"He was a laid-back guy and it just suited us," said first baseman Cecil Cooper. "We didn't need a guy panicking and punching buttons. We knew how to play the game. We put the hit-and-run on

DID YOU KNOW . . . Reliever Dwight Bernard allowed only four homers in 79 innings pitched in 1982, the best ratio (one every 19.2 IP) on the pitching staff.

ourselves, things like that. Harvey didn't have a big ego. Really, he was the perfect guy. It was like the switch turned on when he took over. It was phenomenal from that point on. That was the real key to our season."

The Brewers took off like a bunch of wild horses under the loose rein of Kuenn. They won 20 of 27 games in June, setting an American League record over one stretch by socking 35 home runs over a remarkable 15-game stretch. Known as "Bambi's Bombers" a few years earlier under manager George Bamberger, the free-swinging club took on a new nickname that fit like a thousand-dollar suit. "Harvey's Wallbangers" continued to pound balls out of sight, tearing through enemy pitchers without mercy.

Shortstop Robin Yount, already an eight-year veteran at age 26, became a full-fledged star with a fabulous season at the plate. Yount led the league with 210 hits, 367 total bases, a .578 slugging percentage, and 46 doubles. At season's end, Yount was an easy choice for Most Valuable Player in the league, finishing with a .331 batting average, 29 home runs, and 114 RBIs.

Yount already had formed a tight bond with Kuenn, the hitting coach. As time passed, Yount discovered his batting style was similar to the one Kuenn used to bat .303 over 15 seasons in the majors, including a robust .353 for Detroit in 1959 to win the American League batting title.

"From what I understood and what other people told me, there were similarities in our offensive approach to hitting," Yount said. "He used to hit the ball to right-center, too. Maybe he saw that and took a liking to me. I didn't know much about him as a player, except for his name. He was always talking to me, from the very beginning, talking hitting.

"He taught me how to play the game, basically. It was more than just the hitting of a baseball. He was a play-hard-all-the-time type guy, which was how I felt the game was supposed to be played, too. I

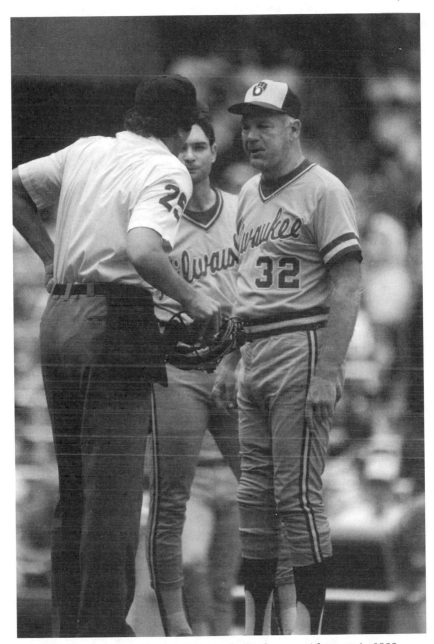

No-nonsense manager Harvey Kuenn, who took over midseason in 1982, wasn't afraid to tell his players, coaches, or even the umpires exactly what he thought. Photo courtesy of Getty Images.

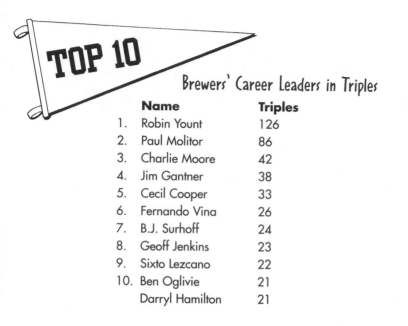

TOP 10

Brewers' Career Leaders in Triples

	Name	Triples
1.	Robin Yount	126
2.	Paul Molitor	86
3.	Charlie Moore	42
4.	Jim Gantner	38
5.	Cecil Cooper	33
6.	Fernando Vina	26
7.	B.J. Surhoff	24
8.	Geoff Jenkins	23
9.	Sixto Lezcano	22
10.	Ben Oglivie	21
	Darryl Hamilton	21

respected him so much that whenever he said something I took it to heart. If he said this was the way something was supposed to be done, in my opinion that was the way it was supposed to be done. That's how much I respected him."

Yount also admired the way Kuenn handled personal adversity, including a series of health problems that included heart bypass surgery, kidney and stomach ailments, and a loss of blood circulation that led to the amputation of his right leg in 1980.

"He had been through about all you could go through in the game of baseball, and off the field, too," Yount said. "Throughout all of that, he was always the same guy, which is what you hear about good people. You could never tell whether he was having a good day or a bad day. He was always the same guy, and a very successful one at that and one I respected immensely."

As might be expected, that relationship changed somewhat when Kuenn replaced Rodgers as the Brewers' manager.

"He really couldn't be one of the guys after that because he was the manager," Yount said. "But you knew if you gave him your very best effort he would go down fighting with you. That's all he expected out of you. Nobody even thought of not giving him your full effort because we all respected him so much and knew it wasn't acceptable not to give your full effort."

That combined effort led to a 72–43 record with Kuenn at the helm, resulting in a league-best 95–67 record and the AL East crown. Kuenn was named AL Manager of the Year for turning the club around and leading it to its first pennant. The Brewers accomplished that feat the hard way, falling behind two games to none in the best-of-five league championship series before rallying for three consecutive victories over the stunned California Angels.

Born in the Milwaukee suburb of West Allis, Kuenn was truly one of their own and a beloved figure among the club's loyal following. Kuenn and wife Audrey owned a motel and bar called Cesar's, a popular local hangout that gained national attention during the Brewers' march to the World Series. A devoted golfer and bowler, Kuenn would sit patiently in the corner of the dugout during games, a monstrous wad of chewing tobacco bulging out his cheek.

Following the lead of their manager, the Brewers were a team of grit. Despite arm problems late in the season, right-hander Pete Vuckovich won 18 games, including a pair of eight-game winning streaks, to claim the AL Cy Young Award. Fan favorite "Stormin'" Gorman Thomas whacked 39 homers and drove in 112 runs. Ben Oglivie and Cooper each hit more than 30 homers and drove in more than 100 runs. Ted Simmons had a great year behind the plate, committing only three errors and knocking in 97 runs.

"Harvey's Wallbangers" could not be stopped, sending a whopping 891 runners across the plate.

TRIVIA

What were the four offensive categories in which Robin Yount led the American League as MVP in 1982?

Answers to the trivia questions are on page 147.

"Harvey just made out the lineup and got out of the way," said Yount. "We had a pretty solid eight guys that you could throw out there every day. Harvey was our leader and we respected him. Whatever he said, there were no questions asked. Harvey had been there a long time. He was a staple of the organization. We believed in what he said."

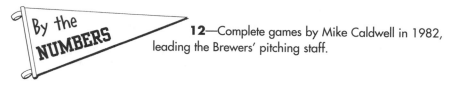

12—Complete games by Mike Caldwell in 1982, leading the Brewers' pitching staff.

The '82 Brewers were a close-knit bunch, on and off the field.

"We'd have team parties and everybody would show up," said third baseman/designated hitter Don Money. "We went out together on the road. We'd sit around in the clubhouse after games and talk baseball. You might just pick up one thing that could help you.

"We had a lot of characters on that team. Vuckie and Gorman, Gantner, Robin. It looked like people left everyday jobs and came to work at the ballpark. They had the long hair and moustaches. But people loved it. It was a blue-collar city and the fans were great to us."

What was not to love? The Brewers finally made it to the World Series, though it ended in heartbreaking fashion with a seven-game defeat at the hands of the St. Louis Cardinals. But it was a season to remember, with the turning point coming on June 2 in Seattle, when Kuenn held his mini-meeting and told the boys to go get 'em.

"That meeting probably lasted about three minutes," said Cooper. "We had a lot of characters on that team. We were a real loose bunch. Harvey just let us play. It was a perfect fit."

Now or Never

If there was ever a time for a team to push the collective panic button, the final day of the 1982 season was it. The Brewers went into their season-ending, four-game series in Baltimore needing only one victory to eliminate the Orioles and finally claim their first American League East title.

Yet, in what amounted to a colossal pratfall, the Brewers dropped the first three games of the series to allow Baltimore to draw even and set up a winner-take-all finale for the division crown. And the Orioles did it in convincing fashion, outscoring the Brewers by a whopping 26–7 margin over the first three games. If the Brewers dropped the final game, they would have been known forever as one of the worst final-weekend gaggers in big-league history.

Yet, to look around the visiting clubhouse at Memorial Stadium on that Sunday morning, one would have thought it was any other day. There was no wringing of hands, no gnashing of teeth, no outward signs that anything had gone amiss.

The previous night, after absorbing an 11–3 shellacking by the Orioles, third baseman Sal Bando, the team captain, took a large group of players out to eat in Baltimore's Little Italy. It was an effort to ease the tension, to have some fun, to rally together one last time and go out in a blaze of glory the following day.

Right-hander Don Sutton remembered the gathering for one reason in particular.

"Sal was buying," recalled Sutton, who drew the starting assignment for the critical season-ender. "That in itself was an event. I figured if that miracle could happen on Saturday night, another one could take place on Sunday. We might have had a bottle of wine or three."

TOP 10

The leaders in runs scored for the Brewers in 1982, when they led the American League in that category with 891 as a team.

	Name	Runs
1.	Paul Molitor	136
2.	Robin Yount	129
3.	Cecil Cooper	104
4.	Gorman Thomas	96
5.	Ben Oglivie	92
6.	Ted Simmons	73
7.	Charlie Moore	53
8.	Jim Gantner	48
9.	Don Money	40
10.	Roy Howell	31

It was only fitting that Sutton took the mound for the do-or-die game against the Orioles. In a brilliant move in late August, general manager Harry Dalton acquired Sutton from Houston for Kevin Bass, Frank DiPino, and Mike Madden in an effort to push the Brewers over the top. It was a deal that energized the club and excited Sutton from the moment he heard the news.

"When the trade was made, I told my family, 'We're going to the World Series,'" said Sutton. "I had watched that ball club. I knew the talent they had."

In the hours before he started a game, Sutton preferred to be by himself, and he wasn't about to change that routine on this day. He rose early and went to the restaurant at the team hotel, the Cross Keys Inn, for a quiet breakfast. As Sutton sat at his table, reading the local newspaper, he felt a presence over his shoulder.

It was none other than the venerable Howard Cosell, part of the television broadcast crew for the game that day.

"Well, it's a big one today," boomed Cosell in his baritone voice, sitting down across from Sutton without invitation. "How are you feeling about going against Palmer?"

"Have you asked Palmer how he feels about going against me?" replied Sutton.

Touché. While the Orioles felt very secure in having future Hall of Famer Jim Palmer on the hill that day, the Brewers were equally confident in their Cooperstown-bound pitcher. And Sutton was confident he would get the job done as well. In fact, he was so calm that morning it was rather scary.

"Through it all, I felt completely at ease," Sutton recalled. "I wasn't even thinking about who was going to be the hero or who was going to step up and do what. I just had a sense that it was going to turn out all right. I felt privileged to have that ballgame. I felt privileged to have the responsibility. I just had a feeling it was going to turn out well for us."

Three days earlier, when the Brewers arrived in Baltimore, Sutton was suffering from a respiratory bug. He was given antibiotics but had an allergic reaction to the medication and broke out in hives. The next day, he received a cortisone injection to counteract the shot of antibiotics. Sometimes, as they say, the cure is worse than the disease.

Sutton was feeling okay again when he reported to the ballpark Sunday. He ducked into the trainer's room to get his right big toe and left heel taped, measures he had used for weeks to combat nagging injuries. While trainers addressed those needs, shortstop Robin Yount ducked in and surprised Sutton by sticking a finger in his chest.

"Don't make us score five runs to get even and we'll kick his butt!" said Yount, who later that day would play a major role in the outcome of the game.

Because Yount was a quiet, soft-spoken and very even-keeled player who rarely made such proclamations, Sutton was stunned. And duly impressed.

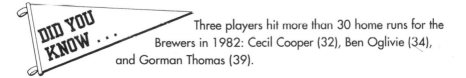

DID YOU KNOW . . . Three players hit more than 30 home runs for the Brewers in 1982: Cecil Cooper (32), Ben Oglivie (34), and Gorman Thomas (39).

"I felt like I wasn't just pitching for the Brewers. I was pitching for the whole state of Wisconsin," recalled Don Sutton of his win over the Orioles to clinch the American League East in 1982. Photo courtesy of Getty Images.

"Robin had never said anything like that," said Sutton. "The way he articulated it was very important. I can still hear him saying it."

The next visitor was manager Harvey Kuenn, another man of few words. If Kuenn's mission was to test the temperature of Sutton's mood, any anxiety he might have had was quickly diminished.

"Well, 'Arch,' what are you going to do today?" asked Sutton, using the nickname that most players used for their beloved leader.

"I'm going to cross my good leg over my bad leg, sit in my corner of the dugout and watch an old pro go to work," Kuenn replied in matter-of-fact fashion.

And thus, the stage was set for one of the greatest days in franchise history. As Milwaukee's team bus approached Memorial Stadium, fans lined up on both sides of the street, waving brooms and yelling, "Sweep! Sweep!" But there would be no sweep. If the Orioles expected the Brewers to roll over after getting blown away in the first three games of the series, they were sadly mistaken.

"It was kind of a surreal scene," said third baseman Paul Molitor. "I don't recall being overly nervous that day. Concerned, yeah. This was just baseball. It doesn't get any better. You're playing one game to get to the playoffs."

There was one nervous Nellie in the traveling party, however. Team president/owner Bud Selig, a noted pacer and worrier, could barely sleep the previous night. For the first time in his 13 years with the club, Selig asked Kuenn if he could address the players before the game. His message was simple.

"All I told them was that I was very proud of them and I thanked them for everything," Selig said. "I just said, 'Go out there and have some fun.'"

TRIVIA

Two pitchers tied for second on the Brewers staff with six saves apiece behind Rollie Fingers' team-high 29 in 1982. Who were they?

Answers to the trivia questions are on page 147.

That's exactly what the Brewers did, and the previously sky-high Orioles never had a chance. Yount socked two homers and a triple, Sutton thoroughly out-pitched Palmer, and left fielder Ben Oglivie made a rally-killing, highlight-reel catch in the eighth inning, sliding into the corner to rob Joe

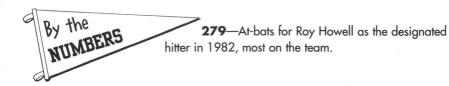

279—At-bats for Roy Howell as the designated hitter in 1982, most on the team.

Nolan of at least a double with two men on base and the Brewers clinging to a 5–2 lead.

The Brewers blew open the game with five runs in the top of the ninth, resulting in a 10–2 whipping of the stunned Orioles and touching off a wild celebration in the visiting clubhouse.

"It was bedlam, absolute bedlam," said Sutton. "That's what you play for. I felt so privileged and gratified to have the ball the last day, and have it turn out well. I felt like I wasn't just pitching for the Brewers. I was pitching for the whole state of Wisconsin."

It was exactly what Dalton had in mind when he swung the trade for Sutton in late August. There was no way of knowing at the time that Sutton would have to win on the final day of the season to make the playoffs, but it was a fitting finish to a dream season.

"Sutton was our savior," said Cooper. "It was almost like it was meant to be for him to be on the mound that day. I just knew he was going to do something like that. He was the difference-maker."

California Dreamin'

As the weary yet exhilarated Brewers traveled cross-country from their division-clinching game in Baltimore on the final day of the 1982 season, they almost didn't need an airplane to get to Anaheim, California. That's how high they were flying after winning their first AL East championship.

But a not-so-funny thing happened to the Brewers as they took the field against the California Angels to battle for their first pennant. They came out flatter than the proverbial pancake.

The Angels took it to 17-game winner Mike Caldwell in Game 1, rolling to an 8–3 victory. When California toppled soon-to-be-named Cy Young Award winner Pete Vuckovich in Game 2, 4–2, the Brewers were all but done. After all, no club ever had extricated itself from a 0–2 hole in LCS play.

"The series in Baltimore was so emotional," said shortstop Robin Yount, the AL MVP that season. "We flew clear across the country to California and came out flat. It took everything we had to beat the Orioles and we kind of lost the emotional edge. It felt like we weren't as ready to play when we got to California. We didn't do much in those first two games."

The sagging Brewers returned to Milwaukee, hoping the friendly surroundings of County Stadium would give them a jump start. But they didn't kid themselves. They knew they were in trouble. At that point, the Brewers had lost six of seven games, the one exception the season-ending, division-clinching victory in Baltimore.

"I don't think we had a lot of confidence at that point," admitted Yount. "We were holding on by a thread. But all it takes is one win, and then you never know."

The Brewers got that "one win" in Game 3, toppling the Angels, 5–3, in front of a raucous home crowd of 50,135. Veteran right-hander Don Sutton, who prevented a monumental collapse in Baltimore by beating the Orioles on the final day of the regular season, came through again. Paul Molitor chipped in with his second homer of the series, and just like that, the Brewers' collective pulse grew stronger.

"We had to win one game first," said Sutton. "You can't think at that point about winning three in a row. It might be a cliché, but you have to play them one game at a time in a situation like that."

The Brewers were energized by their home fans, who hadn't seen them play at County Stadium in a week and a half. They weren't fazed when Angels manager Gene Mauch decided to start left-hander Tommy John in Game 4, a day ahead of schedule. The

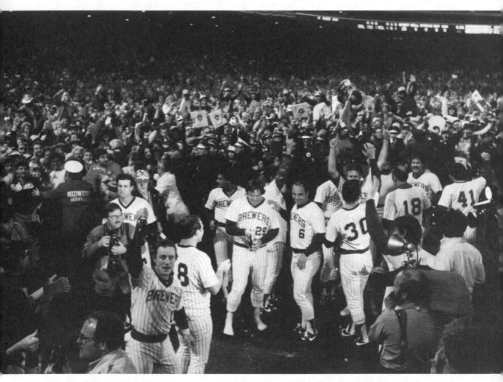

Fans of the Milwaukee Brewers crowded the field after the Brewers defeated the California Angels in the fifth game of the American League playoffs in 1982. Photo courtesy of Bettman/CORBIS.

Brewers got to John for three runs in the second inning, broke open the game with three more in the fourth, and cruised to a 9–5 victory over the now-reeling Angels.

TRIVIA

How many games did Don Sutton win in seven starts with the Brewers in 1982 after being acquired from Houston on August 30?

Answers to the trivia questions are on page 147.

Mauch, criticized in 1964 for shortening his pitching rotation as the Philadelphia Phillies blew a six and one-half game lead with 12 to play to lose the NL pennant to St. Louis, had gambled with his staff and lost again. He figured a sinker-ball pitcher like John wouldn't be adversely affected by the short rest but was wrong. And this was no time to be wrong.

"His ball wasn't sinking as much and we ended up beating him," said designated hitter Don Money. "And we couldn't beat him (before that)."

Just like that, the Brewers had drawn even in the series and now had the home-field advantage firmly on their side. October 10, a gray Sunday afternoon, became a day to remember as a record crowd of 54,968 squeezed into County Stadium to watch their heroes make history.

"When we tied the series, the pressure was squarely on their shoulders," said first baseman Cecil Cooper, who would carve out a place in franchise lore before the day was done.

Just because they had allowed the Brewers to draw even in the series didn't mean the Angels were ready to roll over. The visitors took a 3–2 lead into the bottom of the seventh, when things suddenly began to turn in favor of the Brewers. It started with one out on a blooper near second base by Charlie Moore off Luis Sanchez that second baseman Bobby Grich was ruled to have trapped after some discussion among the umpires.

Taking advantage of that break, the Brewers put together a rally. Jim Gantner followed with a sharp single up the middle. Paul Molitor popped out but Robin Yount drew a walk to load the bases. That brought to the plate Cooper, a missing link in the series with only two hits in 19 at-bats, not to mention a defensive gaffe on a bunt play earlier in the game that led to the go-ahead run for California.

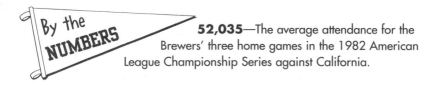

52,035—The average attendance for the Brewers' three home games in the 1982 American League Championship Series against California.

Cooper had whiffed with two runners aboard in the fifth inning, but none of that mattered now. As he stepped to the plate, the crowd greeted him with their customary chant: "Cooooop! Cooooop!" Before leaving the on-deck circle, Cooper glanced into the stands and made eye contact with his wife, Octavia. She motioned to him that he was going to get a hit.

Mauch had left-hander Andy Hassler warming up in the bullpen, presumably to call upon should the left-handed-hitting Cooper come to the plate. But, in yet another pitching decision that left him open to second-guessing and ridicule, Mauch stuck with Sanchez, a 29-year-old Venezuelan in his second year in the majors.

"I assumed he was bringing Hassler in," said Cooper. "He was ready and he was a tough guy to face. He left Sanchez in. I didn't expect that."

Sanchez quickly got two strikes on Cooper, putting him in a defensive mode at the plate. When Sanchez came back with a fast-ball on the outer half, Cooper jumped out of his pronounced crouch and slapped it into left field for an opposite-field single. Moore scored standing up from third and Gantner raced around from second, sliding in with the go-ahead run as the standing-room-only throng roared its approval.

"Charlie jumped on my back," said Gantner. "He was excited. I was excited. But I told him, 'We've still got to get six outs.'"

"All I was trying to do was put the ball in play," said Cooper. "When I saw that thing starting to sink, that's what you dream about. That moment. The noise was deafening, unbelievable. The people were going berserk. I was kind of flying at the time.

"I don't remember getting chill bumps or anything. I think I was more grateful than anything because I had a chance to put us ahead a couple of innings before and didn't do it. The only thing was it wasn't in the bottom of the ninth. That would have been the perfect scenario."

Manager Harvey Kuenn had sent young reserve Marshall Edwards to center field to replace gimpy-kneed Gorman Thomas in the top of the seventh. The move turned out to be a stroke of genius an inning later. California slugger Don Baylor sent a drive to deep center that had extra-base hit written all over it, but Edwards raced back and made an electrifying, leaping catch against the wall.

"I never made a better play in that kind of situation, but then I've never been in that kind of situation before," Edwards later said with a wry smile.

The Brewers had been getting by since the end of July without closer Rollie Fingers, the 1981 AL MVP and Cy Young Award winner who tore a muscle in his elbow and was lost for the remainder of the season. Kuenn, who tried a variety of pitchers to close games, opted for big right-hander Pete Ladd to finish off the Angels after Bob McClure gave up a single to Ron Jackson to lead off the ninth. Ladd, who spent the first half of the season at Class AAA Vancouver, retired the next two batters on a sacrifice and a ground ball. Jackson, the potential tying run, was now on second with two down in the top of the ninth.

Standing between the Brewers and their first pennant was none other than Rod Carew, future Hall of Famer and one of the toughest

TOP 10

Most Victories in a Month

	Record	Month/Year
1.	21–9	June 1978
2.	20–7	September 1992
	20–7	June 1982
4.	20–8	July 1983
5.	20–13	August 1983
6.	19–10	July 1979
	19–10	August 1991
8.	19–11	August 1982
9.	19–13	June 1975
10.	18–3	April 1987

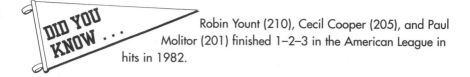

Robin Yount (210), Cecil Cooper (205), and Paul Molitor (201) finished 1–2–3 in the American League in hits in 1982.

outs in the game. Club president Bud Selig, sitting next to Don Drysdale, turned to the pitching great turned broadcaster and said, "Why him? Of all people, why does it have to be him?"

Pouncing out of his own trademark crouch, Carew sent a shot to the left side that was struck sharply but right at Yount, who gobbled it up on a hop and threw across to Cooper for the pennant-clinching out. At long last, the Brewers were going to the World Series.

A city that hadn't witnessed a baseball championship since the '57 Braves won the National League pennant partied into the wee hours of the morning. Fans drove back and forth through downtown on Wisconsin Avenue, honking their horns and screaming until they were hoarse. Players tried to get their cars out of the parking lot at County Stadium with absolutely no luck.

"I had to walk back to where I was staying," said Sutton. "You couldn't even get on Wisconsin Avenue, with all the people celebrating."

Emotional club president Bud Selig got home at 1:00 AM to find his wife asleep. He turned on his radio and heard a voice say, "And in the 1982 World Series, it will be the St. Louis Cardinals versus the Milwaukee Brewers."

"I looked at my little black radio and cried," he said.

The Suds Series

It was quickly billed as "The Suds Series," for obvious reasons. The Brewers came from a town known for brewing beer. The St. Louis Cardinals were owned by the legendary beer barons of Anheuser Busch. The 1982 World Series figured to be eventful and fun, for many reasons.

Game 1 was anything but fun for the Cardinals, however. Using the momentum they built in winning the final three games of the American League Championship Series against California, the Brewers steamrolled the Cardinals, 10–0, in Busch Stadium. *Is the World Series supposed to be this easy?* some of the Brewers wondered.

Left-hander Mike Caldwell, who was roughed up by the Angels in the opener of the ALCS, dominated the Cardinals, tossing a three-hitter. Leadoff hitter Paul Molitor singled five times in six at-bats, becoming the first player in the 79-year history of the fall classic to collect five hits in a game.

"In the third or fourth inning, I played the infield in," Cardinals manager Whitey Herzog said after the game. "The way [Caldwell] was pitching, I figured we'd be lucky to get two or three runs."

The way Caldwell was pitching, two or three runs would have been an absolute bonanza. He retired 17 of the first 18 hitters and the Cardinals were never in the game.

"I'd probably have to consider this one of my best performances this year, and probably my career, since this is the World Series," said the understated, humble Caldwell.

It was a different story in Game 2 for the Brewers, who felt they gift-wrapped the Cardinals' 5–4 victory. That's what happens when you beat yourself with a bases-loaded walk.

Brewers reliever Bob McClure figured in four decisions during the '82 World Series, saving two of his team's three victories and getting the loss in two of their four defeats.

Pete Ladd, the rookie right-hander who filled the closer's role vacated when Rollie Fingers tore a muscle in his forearm, took over for Bob McClure in the eighth inning with two on, one out, and the score tied, 4–4. After a close 3–2 pitch to Lonnie Smith was called ball four by umpire Bill Haller, Ladd lost his composure.

"I did, and it cost us the game," he admitted afterward.

Ladd missed the strike zone badly with all four pitches he threw to pinch-hitter Steve Braun, allowing George Hendrick to trot across with the eventual winning run. The Brewers talked afterward about the close pitch to Smith, but manager Harvey Kuenn, never one for excuses, refused to blame the loss on the umpire.

"You can't blame one call for losing the game," said the stoic Kuenn. Catcher Ted Simmons agreed: "Ball four on Braun is what beat us. Ball four on Lonnie Smith did not."

There was also the matter of blowing an early 3–0 lead, an unexpected turn of events with veteran right-hander Don Sutton on the mound. Sutton propelled the Brewers into the playoffs by beating Baltimore on the final day of the season and was magnificent against the California Angels in the ALCS. On this day, however, he didn't have it.

Sutton would come up empty again in critical Game 6 as the Cardinals rolled to a 13–1 victory that evened the Series.

"I ran out of gas," admitted Sutton, whose acquisition with two months to go was the difference-maker in the Brewers' pennant push. "As much as it pains a professional to say it, I had pitched a lot of innings in September and October and I flat ran out of gas. I regret that to this day. I regret I didn't have 'younger' innings to give to the Brewers."

Play shifted to Milwaukee for Game 3 as delirious Brewers fans got their first taste of the electric atmosphere of the World Series. But that taste quickly turned sour as the Cardinals rolled to a 6–2 victory behind a pair of homers from unlikely slugger Willie McGee.

McGee, a rookie outfielder with a lanky frame and facial features that led to the nickname "E.T.," hit only four homers during the regular season. That didn't stop him from going deep twice off Brewers ace Pete Vuckovich.

"A guy hits four home runs all year, you won't expect him to hit two in a game," Vuckovich said with disgust after the game. "But he did."

On the flip side, the Brewers were no match for the blazing fast-ball of Joaquin Andujar, who kept them off the scoreboard until he was literally knocked out of the game in the seventh inning. Brewers catcher Ted Simmons sent a one-hop shot up the middle that caromed off Andujar's right leg just below the knee. Andujar writhed on the ground in pain before being led from the field.

"I was just glad it didn't hit Andujar in the head or some place where it would hurt him real bad," Simmons said. As the Brewers

Mike Caldwell raises his arms in victory after the Brewers defeated the St. Louis Cardinals in the first game of the 1982 World Series in St. Louis. Photo courtesy of Bettman/CORBIS.

would discover oh-so-painfully in Game 7, Andujar was anything but finished in the World Series.

McGee didn't limit his heroics to two homers. With a runner on and nobody out in the bottom of the ninth, Brewers slugger Gorman Thomas sent a pitch from St. Louis closer Bruce Sutter to deep left-center. Thinking for sure he had socked a homer that would close the gap to two runs, Thomas went into his trot out of the batter's box. "I thought it was out," he said.

And it would have been if not for McGee, who raced back, leaped, and reached over the fence to snatch back Thomas's would-be homer. It was that kind of night for "E.T." McGee.

The Brewers always seemed to play better in the face of adversity, so there was no panic when they fell behind, two games to one. Sure enough, they won Games 4 and 5 before ecstatic audiences at County Stadium to take a 3–2 series lead and put them one game away from taking home the big trophy.

Game 4 was eventful for Thomas, to say the least. Things weren't looking promising for either the Brewers or "Stormin' Gorman" in the first two-thirds of the game, as the Cardinals roared to a 5–1 lead. Thomas suffered the ultimate indignation in the second inning when he fell on the seat of his pants after catching a deep drive by Tommy Herr, allowing the first two-run sacrifice fly in World Series history.

TRIVIA

Who hit the most home runs for the Brewers in the 1982 World Series?

Answers to the trivia questions are on page 147.

When Thomas popped out to open the bottom of the seventh, extending a prolonged slump in which he collected only five hits in 59 at-bats, he heard a new sound from the County Stadium stands. "Boooo! Boooo!" Thomas, who had quickly become a fan favorite with blue-collar Brewers fans with his beer-drinking, every-man approach to life and baseball, was actually being booed by the frustrated faithful. His teammates were stunned.

"You don't hear that," said Jim Slaton, the Game 4 winning pitcher. "Not with Gorman."

Thomas would get a second chance in what became a six-run rally, and there would be no boos this time around. He capped the

TOP 10

Most Hits Collected in a Season

	Hits	Name	Year
1.	219	Cecil Cooper	1980
2.	216	Paul Molitor	1991
3.	210	Robin Yount	1982
4.	205	Cecil Cooper	1982
5.	203	Cecil Cooper	1983
6.	201	Paul Molitor	1982
7.	198	Jeff Cirillo	1999
	198	Fernando Vina	1998
	198	Robin Yount	1987
9.	195	Paul Molitor	1992
	195	Robin Yount	1989

winning outburst with a two-run single, later flashing his devilish sense of humor after helping the Brewers draw even with the Cardinals with a 7–5 victory.

"I started the inning with a pop-up to the catcher," he said. "Hey, you could say I started the winning rally."

Game 5 required another late rally for the Brewers, whose never-say-die attitude was evident once again. It was a nine-inning battle, especially for Caldwell, the veteran lefty who blanked the Cardinals on three hits in Game 1. This time, St. Louis peppered Caldwell for 14 hits in eight and one-third innings. It was a classic example of a pitcher who would bend but not break.

"I'm more proud of this one than the one I pitched the other day," Caldwell said after the 6–4 victory, secured by makeshift closer McClure in the ninth.

"It meant a lot to me," Caldwell continued. "But it will mean a lot more after we've won the fourth game."

Unfortunately for the Brewers, that fourth victory never came. There was no way to know that after yet another come-from-behind triumph in Game 5, paced by Robin Yount's second four-hit performance of the Series and several fielding gems from Caldwell's

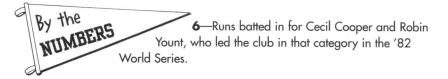

By the NUMBERS

6—Runs batted in for Cecil Cooper and Robin Yount, who led the club in that category in the '82 World Series.

supporting cast. The Brewers even managed to score a couple of runs off Sutter, the Cardinals' previously impenetrable closer.

"We really thought we were going to win that Series after we won Game 5," recalled second baseman Jim Gantner. "We had the momentum on our side. We knew we still had one to go. We still had to win one more, but everybody was really confident we were going to win."

When action moved back to Busch Stadium in St. Louis, things took an ugly turn for the Brewers. They were blown out from start to finish in Game 6, getting pummeled, 13–1, in a brilliant performance by St. Louis starter John Stuper. Adding to that insult, Commissioner Bowie Kuhn refused to shorten a World Series game when torrential rains hit in the sixth inning with the Cardinals leading, 8–0. The Brewers were forced to endure a two-hour, 13-minute delay before absorbing the rest of their error-filled humiliation.

The Brewers won a do-or-die game in Baltimore on the final day of the season to clinch the division. They won three more in the ALCS after falling behind, two games to none, to California. Now, one last time, they were confronted with another elimination game.

"We've been in this position before," Don Money said before the game. "Every week, for the last four weeks, it's been the same thing. I guess we've got them right where we want them."

But Money guessed wrong. The final game would not go the Brewers' way this time. The Cardinals showed they were just as comeback worthy, rallying from a 3–1 deficit to take Game 7, 6–3, breaking the hearts of the Brewers and their fans. Andujar, who had tormented the Brewers in Game 3 before being knocked from the game by Simmons's shot, came through again before turning it over to Sutter.

The Brewers were without their closer, Fingers. But the Cardinals had the ever-reliable split-finger fastball of Sutter, who retired the final six hitters in order, striking out Thomas to end it.

"Our whole plan in that Series was to get the lead early to stay away from Sutter," Gantner said. "We didn't want to face him with that 'splitter.' He was really tough. We wanted to get the lead early and keep him out of the game as much as we could."

Had Fingers pitched the eighth inning of Game 2 instead of Ladd, the Series might not have made it back to St. Louis for the final two games. It was a maddening game of "What if?" that is still debated in Milwaukee to this very day.

"I don't know if I would have made a difference," said Fingers. "But I will say this. I would have liked to have been there to try."

Born to be Wild

When the disheartened Brewers returned to Milwaukee after losing the '82 World Series to St. Louis, they were flabbergasted by the response from their beloved city and its loyal fans. Treating their fallen heroes like world champions, city officials staged a parade through the heart of downtown on Wisconsin Avenue, ending with a rally at County Stadium.

Many players had to be talked into attending. They weren't in the mood to celebrate after losing the last two games in St. Louis, watching their dreams get dashed. But their spirits were lifted by the tremendous outpouring of love from the city's baseball fans.

"I remember how down I was," pitcher Jim Slaton said. "My first feeling was that I didn't want to go. I think everybody was mentally drained. But to see the way the fans reacted around town was very gratifying and uplifting.

"I've been in a lot of places, just about every baseball town, and I can't think of any place better than Milwaukee was."

No player was in a darker mood than shortstop Robin Yount, who a few weeks later would be named MVP of the American League. Yount took the World Series defeat particularly hard, and now they wanted him to put on a happy face and take part in a runners-up parade? It didn't make sense to Yount, for whom winning meant everything.

"I was devastated that we didn't win the World Series," said Yount. "It's the goal for your whole life, and you don't quite get it. You work so hard to get there and you get so close and lose. It hurts. I was so depressed."

To help clear his head, Yount decided to ride his motorcycle to County Stadium, where the team had gathered to prepare for the

parade through downtown. He was informed the festivities would conclude with a rally at the ballpark.

"I was kind of being a rebel or whatever," he said. "That motorcycle wasn't even street legal, but for whatever reason I had it in Milwaukee all year. It was just a dirt bike.

"I rode this dirt bike through the streets of Milwaukee. It didn't even have license plates. I didn't care if I got pulled over. It just didn't matter. Nothing mattered at that time.

"I was still so mad that morning, knowing we had to go to the ballpark and go through this parade. I really didn't want to do that. But it ended up being a great thing."

Indeed, it did. After the team returned to County Stadium for the rally, Pete Vuckovich, Gorman Thomas, and Ted Simmons spotted Yount's motorcycle parked in the underground tunnel. The mischievous trio urged Yount to ride the bike onto the field when he was announced to the crowd. Yount initially balked at the idea but eventually said, "What the heck."

With some 20,000 fans in the stands, the players were introduced, one by one, and walked onto the field. But when Yount's name was called, he was nowhere to be seen. Suddenly, the bullpen gates opened and out roared a leather-clad rider on a motorcycle, one fist raised in the air. When fans realized it was Yount, they went nuts.

"The Kid" took a lap around the outfield warning track before eventually making his way to home plate, where he slammed on the brakes and dismounted. It was a legendary moment by a legendary player, at least in Milwaukee, an unscripted slice of history destined to go down in club lore.

Brewers designated hitter Roy Howell went hitless in 11 at-bats in the 1982 World Series.

TRIVIA

Who was the Brewers' first-round draft pick in June during their pennant-winning season of 1982?

Answers to the trivia questions are on page 147.

"It just happened out of the clear blue," said Yount. "It wasn't planned. It ended up being something that everybody remembered."

As the crowd continued to roar its approval, team President Bud Selig stood on an infield stage, speechless at what he had just witnessed. He still cringes at the thought of his Hall of Fame shortstop racing around on a motorcycle without wearing a helmet.

"I almost died," said Selig. "Here comes this figure racing around like a mad man, and it's Robin. I can still remember Vuckovich and Simmons saying, 'Don't worry. Your kid will be all right.' I'm up there ready to faint, but the crowd went wild. Nobody knew he was going to do it."

Recognizing Robin Yount's affinity for motorcycles, the Brewers let him ride around County Stadium on a Harley during the closing ceremony in 2000 commemorating the last Major League Baseball game played there. Photo courtesy of AP/Wide World Photos.

TOP 5

Top Five Brewers Hitters in the 1982 World Series

	Name	Average
1.	Robin Yount	.414
2.	Paul Molitor	.355
3.	Charlie Moore	.346
4.	Jim Gantner	.333
5.	Cecil Cooper	.286

Yount, who had ridden motorbikes almost since he was old enough to walk, never imagined his stunt would become so famous. He viewed it as a means of easing the pain of the previous days, when the World Series slipped from the collective grasp of the Brewers.

"It all evolved from the frustration of not winning the World Series," said Yount. "I had this rebel attitude and started doing these things that were pretty out of character. It turned out to be a good thing, I guess."

It had been a year of surprises for the Brewers. A slow start that led to the firing of manager Buck Rodgers and the elevation of hitting Coach Harvey Kuenn. The magical about-face of a hitting machine known as "Harvey's Wallbangers." The final weekend in Baltimore, when the Brewers almost threw it all away with three consecutive losses before a lopsided victory on the last day. The incredible comeback in the ALCS against California. Then, in heartbreaking fashion, the seven-game loss to St. Louis in the World Series.

Yet, the club's adoring fans came out to voice their support, one more time. Not all stories have fairy-tale endings, no matter how captivating. But that didn't shatter the loyalty of the Brewers' following.

"The fans were great in Milwaukee," said first baseman Cecil Cooper. "People just fell in love with our team. We had all these crazy guys, these different characters. We fit right in that atmosphere. All of us were kind of small-city guys."

Mr. Baseball

Bob Uecker's major league career lasted only six years, comprising 297 games as a backup catcher. He compiled a .200 batting average, 14 home runs, and 74 runs batted in, not exactly the kind of numbers you want on the back of your bubble gum card.

Yet, Uecker still made it to the National Baseball Hall of Fame in Cooperstown, New York, in July 2003, 36 years after he retired as a player. How does a career .200 hitter get a bronze plaque in the most hallowed halls in the game? By becoming a legendary radio broadcaster, that's how.

It was Johnny Carson who dubbed Uecker "Mr. Baseball" during one of the broadcaster's many appearances on *The Tonight Show.* Uecker had found his true calling behind a microphone in the Brewers' radio booth in 1971. Given a daily platform to express his unique, self-deprecating, and deadpan brand of humor, Uecker eventually became the face of the franchise, the most recognized personality ever associated with the Brewers.

A native of Milwaukee, Uecker still remembers the day he signed his first professional contract with his hometown Braves.

"I signed for $3,000," Uecker recalled. "That was tough on my dad because he didn't have that kind of dough. But he eventually scraped it up."

And thus began the career of one of the game's true funnymen. A short, undistinguished career, without question, but one that provided an unlimited amount of material for Uecker's ongoing stand-up act. What were his career highlights, you ask?

"I had two," he said. "I got an intentional walk from Sandy Koufax and I got out of a rundown against the Mets.

"I remember one time I was batting against the Dodgers in Milwaukee. They're leading, 2–1, it's the bottom of the ninth, bases loaded, two out and the pitcher has a full count on me. I look over to the Dodger dugout and they're all in street clothes. When I looked at my third base coach, he turned his back on me."

Some players have a difficult time deciding when it's time to retire. According to Uecker, that choice was made for him.

"My baseball card came out and there was no picture on it," he said.

Uecker became a close friend of another Milwaukeean, Bud Selig, who went on to become part owner and president of the Brewers. Shortly after the team began play in Milwaukee in 1970, Uecker asked Selig if there might be a place in the organization for him. Wanting to find something for his buddy to do, Selig made Uecker a scout and sent him to the Northern League to look for players. One day, Brewers general manager Frank Lane barged into Selig's office, screaming something about Uecker.

The beloved "Mr. Baseball," Bob Uecker, throwing out the first pitch at the 2000 home opener in Milwaukee. Photo courtesy of Bettman/CORBIS.

By the
NUMBERS

50—The number of years in baseball, as player and broadcaster, that Bob Uecker celebrated in 2005.

"What's the problem?" asked Selig.

Lane tossed a scouting report from Uecker onto Selig's desk. It was covered with remnants of mashed potatoes and gravy, rendering it virtually unreadable.

"What are we going to do with this guy?" asked Lane.

"I knew then that he wasn't going to make it as a scout, so we decided to try him as a broadcaster," said Selig.

The rest, as they say, is history.

For well over three decades, Uecker has brought Brewers games to life for legions of adoring fans, glued to their radios at home, at work, and in their cars. While beer commercials, network baseball broadcasts, and TV sitcoms, not to mention a trio of baseball movies, brought national fame to Uecker, he always has considered himself the radio voice of the Brewers, first and foremost.

"This is all I ever really wanted to do," said Uecker, who has worked on a handshake agreement since calling his first game. "I never wanted to go anywhere else. I had chances to do other things but I never wanted to leave the Brewers and I never wanted to leave Milwaukee. This is my home.

"I go to the ballpark every day and I have a good time. I can't imagine doing anything else."

Neither can Brewers fans, especially those who have listened faithfully to the team's radio broadcasts. No matter how boring the game, how mundane the action, how meaningless the result, Uecker has kept listeners amused with humorous anecdotes and observations.

"Ueck" was finally recognized nationally for his longtime dedication and service to the Brewers by being named the recipient of the 2003 Ford C. Frick Award, guaranteeing a spot in the broadcast wing of the National Baseball Hall of Fame.

Generally, award recipients are asked to limit their speeches to 10 minutes. Realizing they had the makings of a memorable and hilarious performance, however, Hall of Fame officials told Uecker to take as long as he wanted. The result was a side-splitting, laugh-until-you-cry experience that folks still talk about.

In his trademark deadpan style, Uecker began at the very beginning.

"I was born and raised in Milwaukee, Wisconsin," he said. "Actually, I was born in Illinois. My mother and father were on an oleomargarine run to Chicago back in 1934 because we couldn't get colored margarine in Wisconsin.

"On the way home, my mother was with child—me—and the pain started and my dad pulled off into an exit area, and that's where the event took place. It was a nativity-type setting, an exit light shining down and three truck drivers there. One was carrying butter, one had frankfurters, and the other guy was a retired baseball scout who told my folks that I probably had a chance to play somewhere down the line.

"I remember it being very cold. It was January. I didn't weigh very much—I think the birth certificate says 10 ounces. I was immediately wrapped in swaddling clothes and put in the back of a Chevy without a heater. And that was the start of this Cinderella story that you're hearing today."

Memorable Bob Uecker Quotes

"Anybody with ability can play in the big leagues. But to be able to trick people year in and year out the way I did, I think that was a much greater feat."

"If a guy hits .300 every year, what does he have to look forward to? I always tried to stay around .190, with three or four RBIs. And I tried to get them all in September. That way I always had something to talk about during the winter."

"In 1962, I was named Minor League Player of the Year. It was my second season in the Bigs."

"The biggest thrill a ballplayer can have is when your son takes after you. That happened when my Bobby was in his championship Little League game. He really showed me something. Struck out three times. Made an error that lost the game. Parents were throwing things at our car and swearing at us as we drove off. Gosh, I was proud."

"Sporting goods companies paid me not to endorse their products."

Uecker went on to talk about the tender moments that all ex–big leaguers recall with fondness. At the top of the list was his first big-league game in his hometown of Milwaukee.

"I can remember walking out on the field and Birdie Tebbetts was our manager at that time," recalled Uecker. "And my family was there. My mother and dad, and all my relatives. And as I'm standing on the field, everybody's pointing at me and waving and laughing, and I'm pointing back. And Birdie Tebbetts came up and asked me if I was nervous or uptight about the game.

"And I said, 'I'm not. I've been waiting five years to get here. I'm ready to go.'

"He said, 'Well, we're gonna start you today. I didn't want to tell you earlier. I didn't want you to get too fired up.'

"I said, 'Look, I'm ready to go.'

"He said, 'Well, great, you're in there. And oh, by the by, the rest of us up here wear that supporter on the inside.'

"That was the first game my folks walked out on, too."

Uecker relayed a touching story of playing for the 1964 St. Louis club that won the World Series, and the special request made of him to help the team.

"Bing Devine, who was the Cardinals' general manager at that time, asked me if I would do him and the Cardinals, in general, a favor," recalled Uecker. "And I said I would.

"And he said, 'We'd like to inject you with hepatitis. We need to bring an infielder up.'

"I said, 'Would I able to sit on the bench?'

"He said, 'Yes, we'll build a plastic cubicle for you because it is an infectious disease.'

"And I've got to tell you this. I have a photo at home, I turned a beautiful color of yellow and with that Cardinals white uniform. I was knocked out. It was great."

Uecker talked about his role as the personal catcher for Braves knuckleballer Phil Niekro, and his philosophy for corralling that elusive floater: "Wait until it stops rolling and pick it up."

TRIVIA

What was the name of the character played by Bob Uecker on the hit sitcom *Mr. Belvedere*?

Answers to the trivia questions are on page 147.

DID YOU KNOW . . . Bob Uecker made more than 90 appearances on *The Tonight Show* with Johnny Carson.

And so it went, with the thousands on hand, including living Hall of Famers who nearly fell off the stage with laughter, experiencing the brand of humor that has endeared Uecker to Brewers fans for decades. Never one to take himself too seriously, Uecker remained loyal to his craft, his sport, and, most importantly, his beloved Brewers.

Players have come and gone, good, bad, and everything in between. The one constant has been Uecker, sitting in the radio booth, day after day, season after season, keeping radio broadcasts alive with his insights and uncanny wit. For most Brewers fans, they couldn't imagine tuning into a game and not hearing Uecker's voice.

Uecker's trademark home-run call—"Get up, get up, get out of here! Gone!"—has become such an ingrained part of club history that the Brewers put it in neon lights high atop Miller Park when the new facility opened in 2001.

"To a lot of people, Bob is the Brewers," said Hall of Famer and longtime friend Robin Yount. "Bob has been there from the beginning and he's there every day."

All the King's Men

In professional sports, "dynasties" come and go. Some go faster than others.

Such was the case for the Brewers, who appeared to have the makings of a longtime powerhouse after falling one victory shy of winning the 1982 World Series. In late August 1983, when the Brewers roared into first place in the East Division by winning nine of 11 games, there certainly was no reason to believe their American League reign would be a short one.

But, as quickly as things came together in August, they fell apart in September. The Brewers swooned badly, winning only 10 of 28 games, and when the smoke cleared, they were in fifth place, 11 games behind the Baltimore Orioles. The late-season collapse led to the dismissal of manager Harvey Kuenn, the ultra-popular savior of the 1982 season. It was an unimaginable turn of events for a club that seemed destined to be a power for years to come.

There were many reasons for the Brewers' stunning collapse. Pete Vuckovich, the AL Cy Young Award winner in '82, missed most of the season with a torn rotator cuff and didn't win a game. The burly, gutsy right-hander would never be the same. Ditto for closer Rollie Fingers, who spent the entire year on the disabled list while recovering from elbow surgery.

Other than first baseman Cecil Cooper, who socked 30 homers and drove in a club-record 126 runs, and catcher Ted Simmons, who sent home 108 base runners, nearly every player suffered an offensive drop from the previous season. The team was getting old before the very eyes of general manager Harry Dalton, who tried to do something to change the team's chemistry

TOP 10

Most RBIs in a Season

	RBIs	Name	Year
1.	126	Cecil Cooper	1983
2.	125	Jeromy Burnitz	1998
	125	Richie Sexson	2001
4.	124	Richie Sexson	2003
5.	123	Gorman Thomas	1979
6.	122	Cecil Cooper	1980
7.	121	Cecil Cooper	1982
8.	119	Prince Fielder	2007
9.	118	John Jaha	1996
	118	Ben Oglivie	1980

on June 6 by way of a trade that would rank as the most unpopular in club history.

Dalton sent center fielder Gorman Thomas and pitchers Jamie Easterly and Ernie Camacho to the Cleveland Indians for center fielder Rick Manning and pitcher Rick Waits. Thomas was struggling horribly at the time, batting only .183 with five homers, but was a fan favorite of blue-collar Milwaukee fans and considered the heart and soul of a close-knit bunch that put a premium on togetherness.

"Gorman was a fixture on the team," said infielder/designated hitter Don Money, who was released by the Brewers after the season. "They started dismantling the team pretty quick. They wanted to go another way. New players came in. You didn't have the camaraderie anymore."

Thomas, who loved everything about playing for the Brewers, from the adoring fans to his lifestyle in the city to his close friendship with so many teammates, was devastated when informed of the trade.

"To this day, I still don't understand it," he said. "Baseball wasn't any fun for me after that. I kept playing but it wasn't fun anymore."

As a player, Manning was the polar opposite of the burly Thomas, a slugger whose calling card was the home run. Manning

Though it didn't seem like it at the time for Paul Molitor and the talented Brewers, the 1982 World Series loss to the Cardinals has turned out to be the high-water mark for the team and the franchise so far. Photo courtesy of Bettman/CORBIS.

was a singles hitter whose game was built on speed and defense, and he quickly learned how unpopular the trade was among Thomas's ex-teammates. Reporting to County Stadium after the start of a game, Manning rushed to the home clubhouse to get dressed. There, he stumbled upon Vuckovich, one of Thomas's closest friends.

"I didn't really know him," said Manning. "All I knew from playing against him was he didn't seem like the nicest guy in the world. I went up to introduce myself."

"Hi, I'm Rick Manning," said the newcomer.

"I know," Vuckovich replied. "How the hell did we trade Gorman for you?"

Vuckovich then spun on his heels and walked away, leaving Manning standing there, mouth agape. Welcome to Milwaukee. It was only later that Manning learned that pulling people's chains was a favorite pastime of Vuckovich, a prankster and fun-loving guy under his gruff exterior.

"I said, 'Oh boy, this is going to be a lot of fun,'" recalled Manning. "But that was just Vukie's personality. He was just messing with me.

"I didn't realize how popular Gorman was in Milwaukee until I got there. I told the media, 'I'll never replace Gorman Thomas. I can never be the same guy. Just respect me for who I am.' We were totally opposite players."

Thomas was the first to go of the players around whom the '82 AL championship club was built. Vuckovich spent the entire 1984 season on the disabled list, struggled through an injury-riddled '85 campaign, and retired after the '86 season. Back problems sidelined Fingers for half of 1984 and he was done after a mostly ineffective '85 season. Mike Caldwell, the reliable lefty who won 17 games in '82, slipped to 12 and six victories the next two seasons and also was shown the door. Outfielder Ben Oglivie, a major force on the '82 club with 34 homers and 102 RBIs, began to break down with a series of nagging injuries and never topped 66 RBIs again. Robin Yount's throwing shoulder came apart in 1985, forcing him to move from shortstop to the outfield and robbing him of much of his pop at the plate.

And so it went. One by one, many of the heroes known as "Harvey's Wallbangers" faded from sight. Except for the triumvirate of Yount, Paul Molitor, and Jim Gantner, the team was barely recognizable within a few seasons. Gone were the days when postgame clubhouse card games would go into the wee hours of the night. Players no longer gathered on the field en masse long before batting practice to play spirited games of "flip." The personality of the team had changed, along with the talent level.

"We didn't do stuff that was illegal," Thomas said. "We didn't do things that were bad. We just did things that we enjoyed doing that were clean-cut fun. We did stupid things, but nothing you'd ever be ashamed of.

"Sure, we'd go out and probably drink too much, but everybody did that. Nobody ever showed up late at the ballpark. Nobody ever got in trouble with the law. We had so much fun together. It sounds corny, but it's the gospel truth."

2,397,131—Fans who attended games at County Stadium in 1983, a club attendance record that stood until Miller Park opened in 2001.

But those days were gone. The summer of '84 was a complete disaster, with the Brewers finishing in last place with a 67–94 record, 36½ games behind Detroit. Rookie manager Rene Lachemann never had a chance, but that didn't stop Dalton from sending him packing after one season at the helm.

Dalton tried to turn back time by bringing George Bamberger back to manage the team in 1985, but it was too late. The talent level had slipped too precipitously. The Brewers were only slightly better that season, finishing in sixth place with a 71–90 record. The genie was out of the bottle and there was no putting him back in.

Sure, there were some highlights. Cooper and Molitor made the AL All-Star team in 1985, a season in which lefty Teddy Higuera and shortstop Ernie Riles made impressive big-league debuts. But the Brewers were in serious decline. Almost as quickly as they rose to power in the AL in the early '80s, they sunk back to the depths of the early years of the franchise. All good things come to an end, but nobody expected that inevitability to come so quickly and hit so hard.

"We thought that team would stay together awhile and we'd be back in the World Series," said Cooper. "But it never happened. We kind of fell apart. It seemed like we still had the same team late in '83, but things didn't go our way. That team was so special in 1982. We all got along so well, we had good chemistry. After '83, some of that was missing."

As dynasties go, it was a short-lived one. No one associated with the franchise could have dreamed that the 1982 World Series would be a once-in-a-lifetime experience. The Brewers figured there would be many more falls to remember. Sadly, they were wrong.

TRIVIA

First baseman Cecil Cooper set a club record with 126 RBIs in 1983, tying another player for the major league lead. Who was that player?

Answers to the trivia questions are on page 147.

A Real Teddy Bear

In 1983, Brewers scouting director Ray Poitevint heard about a promising young pitcher in the Mexican League by the name of Teddy Higuera. A somewhat squatty lefty, Higuera was not overpowering but knew how to locate his pitches, had a deceptive, high-kicking delivery, and threw a screwball that bedeviled right-handed hitters.

Poitevint went down to Juarez to take a look at Higuera, liked what he saw, and offered him a contract. Higuera, who spoke little English, was assigned to Class AA El Paso, just across the border from Mexico. Before the year was done, he was pitching for Class AAA Vancouver.

Continuing that rapid ascent, Higuera found himself in the big leagues the next year. The '85 Brewers weren't very good, winning only 71 games under George Bamberger, who agreed to return for a second stint as the club's manager. But Bamberger knew he had a good thing in Higuera, who easily led the club in victories with a 15–8 record. No rookie pitcher had ever won that many games for the Brewers.

Higuera had a bit of a temper, which he allowed to get the best of him at times. But when in control, he was a master on the mound, changing speeds and dissecting baffled hitters who didn't know what was coming next. Folks took notice because Higuera finished second to Chicago's Ozzie Guillen in balloting for AL Rookie of the Year.

"He 'painted' with a thin brush, not a big brush," said catcher Bill Schroeder, who knew an artist when he saw one. "He knew how to pitch. He had a good fastball, but he didn't blow you away. He had one of those 'slower than slow' change-ups. And he'd hit that outside corner with a 'backdoor' curveball and 'four-seamer.' And he was a fierce competitor. If you made a mistake behind him, he'd glare at you."

Higuera quickly established himself as one of the best pitchers in the American League. He won 20 games in 1986, compiling a 2.79 ERA and striking out 207 hitters—a franchise record for left-handers. Higuera finished second in the AL Cy Young Award balloting to Boston ace Roger Clemens, who had the advantage of pitching for a pennant winner. The Brewers won only 77 games, which showed just how dominating Higuera could be on any given day.

TRIVIA

Before Teddy Higuera won 15 games in 1985, who had the Brewers' record for most victories by a rookie?

Answers to the trivia questions are on page 147.

Clemens started for the AL in the All-Star Game that season in Houston and tossed three shutout innings in a 3–2 victory over the NL. Following Clemens to the mound, Higuera was just as dominant, also pitching three shutout frames and allowing only one hit. His performance was overshadowed by fellow countryman Fernando Valenzuela, the Los Angeles Dodgers' phenom who struck out five consecutive hitters to match Carl Hubbell's 52-year-old All-Star Game record. One of Valenzuela's victims was Higuera, who had never batted in a major league game.

In only two seasons in the majors, Higuera had become a full-fledged star. No Brewers pitcher had won 20 games since Mike Caldwell went 22–9 in 1978. Caldwell enjoyed the luxury of pitching for a strong club (93–69). Higuera did not. In the final weeks of the season, manager George Bamberger called it quits, paving the way for third base coach Tom Trebelhorn to take the reins a few days later.

No pitcher in club history has been in a better groove than Higuera during a remarkable three-game stretch in late August and early September of '87. On August 26, he tossed a three-hitter in a 1–0 victory over Cleveland. Next time out, he pitched a masterful one-hitter in Kansas City in a 2–0 triumph. The Mexican marvel then went to Minnesota and hurled a two-hitter to lead the Brewers to a 6–0 victory. Three starts. Six hits allowed. No runs.

Before Higuera's spell was snapped, he pitched a club-record 32 consecutive scoreless innings. It was part of the roller-coaster year of "Team Streak," a nickname given to a club that began the season with a 13–0 record and shortly afterward dropped 12 in a row.

"Those three games were as good as it gets," said Schroeder, who caught the two-hitter against the Twins. "He worked fast. He wanted the ball and he got rid of it. There wasn't a lot of shaking off signs. He knew what he wanted to do."

Teddy Higuera finished second in the American League Cy Young Award balloting to Boston ace Roger Clemens in 1986. Photo courtesy of Getty Images.

Schroeder also experienced the dark side of Higuera's competi-tive nature. In a game that season in New York, Higuera wasn't happy with the target his catcher was providing behind the plate. After one inning in particular, the temperamental lefty came back to the dugout and vigorously complained to Trebelhorn.

"He was bitching and moaning to Treb, saying I wasn't sitting enough on the outside corner," recalled Schroeder. "I said, 'I am on the outside corner! If that's not good enough, get somebody else in there!'

"He finished the game, and we won, and afterward we were all good buddies. What's wrong with that? You can have disagreements out there. I wasn't so sensitive that I put my tail between my legs."

Higuera went 16–9 in 1988, giving him a 69–38 record through four seasons, a stunning winning percentage of .645. Hobbled by back and ankle ailments in 1989, he made only 22 starts and fell off to 9–6. Higuera battled more nagging injuries, mostly to his legs, the following season and finished with an 11–10 record.

That slippage led to a tough decision for general manager Harry Dalton when Higuera became a free agent after the 1990 season. Higuera was being courted by other teams, in particular the San Diego Padres, who had a substantial Hispanic following and figured he would be a perfect fit on their team. Dalton was concerned about the time Higuera missed with injuries the previ-ous two seasons and pondered the dangers of a long-term, big-bucks contract. But Dalton also feared the backlash from Brewers fans if Higuera defected to another team and regained his All-Star form.

After much agonizing, Dalton and club president Bud Selig decided to give Higuera a four-year, $13.1 million contract, by far the biggest in club history. On the night that deal was struck, Dalton was besieged with mixed feelings.

"I didn't know whether to laugh or cry," Dalton said later.

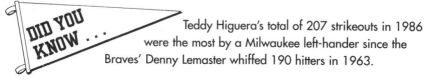

DID YOU KNOW . . . Teddy Higuera's total of 207 strikeouts in 1986 were the most by a Milwaukee left-hander since the Braves' Denny Lemaster whiffed 190 hitters in 1963.

TOP 10

Teddy Higuera's Ranking on the Club's
All-Time Pitching Lists

	Rank	Total
Strikeouts	1st	1,081
Winning Percentage	1st	.595 (94–64)
Victories	3rd	94
Shutouts	3rd	12
Walks	3rd	443
Opp. Batt. Avg.	4th	.243
Games Started	5th	205
Innings Pitched	5th	1,380
Complete Games	5th	50
ERA	3rd	3.61

Much to the dismay of Dalton, Selig, and Higuera, that contract became the most second-guessed and criticized in club history. During training camp the next spring, Higuera tore his rotator cuff, the most dreaded injury for a pitcher. He pitched in only seven games during the '91 season before undergoing major surgery.

Higuera would never be the same. He desperately tried to rehabilitate the shoulder, refusing to give up, but it was no use. After a 1–5 season in 1994 in which he made only 12 starts, Higuera was done. In the three years since signing his big-bucks deal, he won a total of five games. It was a devastating turn of events for the Brewers, who had lost promising young lefty Juan Nieves to a shoulder injury after the '88 season.

Such is life in the big leagues. Pitchers get injured. Was the timing particularly bad in Higuera's case? Of course, but there was nothing the little lefty could do about it. To his credit, Higuera worked endless hours trying to come back from the injury but was left in what Trebelhorn termed a "no pain, no pop" situation. In other words, the shoulder didn't hurt anymore but Higuera could no longer carve up hitters. What made him so special was gone, just like that.

By the NUMBERS 10—The number of games Teddy Higuera won in both the first and second halves of the 1986 season, when he became the third 20-game winner in club history (and, as of 2007, the last).

"People ask me, 'Who's the best pitcher you ever caught?'" said Schroeder. "I caught Bert Blyleven at the end of his career. I caught Chuck Finley. I caught Rollie Fingers and Mike Caldwell. But Teddy Higuera was the best. He dominated.

"When Teddy was on the mound, you knew you were going to win. All you needed was two or three runs. On the rare occasion when he gave up a bunch of runs, you were stunned. Before he got hurt, he was the best."

Team Streak

As the Brewers broke training camp in the spring of 1987, there was little reason to expect something special was about to happen. Yes, there was renewed enthusiasm under new, upbeat manager Tom Trebelhorn, but the team was coming off three consecutive losing seasons and no self-respecting pundit was bold enough to suggest Milwaukee was a team to watch, much less ready to make major league history.

The drama of "Team Streak" was about to unfold.

The Brewers were still a team in transition, with Greg Brock taking over at first base, catcher B.J. Surhoff—the first player taken in the 1985 June draft—coming on board, Dale Sveum claiming the shortstop job, and power-hitting prospect Glenn Braggs getting the nod in right field, with Rob Deer shifting to left. Opening the season at home, the Brewers drew the defending American League champion Boston Red Sox as their first opponent.

But Boston's pitching was in disarray because of injuries, forcing the Red Sox to use Bob Stanley as their Opening Day starter. The Brewers countered with their ace, Teddy Higuera, who pitched the home team to a relatively easy 5–1 victory before 52,585 fans at County Stadium. After the customary off day, the Brewers came back to win the second game, 3–2, with relievers Chuck Crim and Dan Plesac blanking the Red Sox for four innings. The third game was a slugfest, with the Brewers prevailing, 12–11, to complete the opening sweep of the stunned Red Sox.

The Brewers headed off for a six-game trip to Texas and Baltimore, their spirits buoyed by the surprising start. They proceeded to ruin the Rangers' home opener by scoring eight runs in

25—Home runs hit by Dale Sveum in 1987, the most in club history by a switch-hitter.

the first inning en route to an 11–8 victory. Yet another eight-run outburst, this time in the fourth inning, gave Higuera plenty of support as the Brewers won their fifth in a row, 8–6. Victory number six took much more work. The Brewers scored three runs in the eleventh, only to have reliever Mark Clear blow the lead in the bottom of the inning. But a two-run rally in the twelfth secured a 7–5 triumph and the Brewers had their second three-game sweep of opening week.

It was on to Baltimore, where Paul Molitor's hot bat led the way to 6–3 and 7–4 victories over the Orioles. Now 8–0, the Brewers figured it couldn't get much better. But it did, on one of the most memorable evenings in club history.

April 15 was a cold, damp, misty night in Baltimore, and only 11,407 fans ventured to Memorial Stadium. Juan Nieves, who struggled to the 11–8 victory in Texas, was on the mound for the Brewers, taking on Orioles veteran Mike Flanagan. Nieves, a raw but talented 22-year-old lefty beginning his second season in the majors, was a heavily recruited prep star in Connecticut who signed with the Brewers in 1983 for $150,000. The handsome, outgoing native of Puerto Rico was considered to have immense potential, and on this night he showed why.

Surhoff was scheduled to catch Nieves that night but had a root canal procedure earlier in the day and was in no condition to play. During pregame batting practice, Trebelhorn walked up to backup catcher Bill Schroeder.

"Bill, you're catching," said Trebelhorn. "B.J.'s hurting."

It didn't take long for Schroeder to figure out that Nieves's breaking ball wasn't a reliable pitch on this evening. Schroeder found himself putting down his right index finger more and more, calling for Nieves's fastball, which had some giddy-up to it.

"I think we tried about five curveballs, maybe two or three change-ups that were hit hard early in the game," said Schroeder. "After that, it was all 'gas.' He just threw one fastball after another, and they couldn't catch up to it. It was cold and rainy, just miserable, so it wasn't a good night for hitters."

Nieves's defense made some stellar plays in the early going to rob Baltimore hitters. Seldom-used left fielder Jim Paciorek, playing deep with slugger Eddie Murray at the plate in the second, charged in and made a diving catch of a shallow pop fly. Third baseman Molitor snared liners by Cal Ripken Jr. in the fourth inning and Floyd Rayford in the fifth.

With the Brewers clinging to a 1–0 lead, courtesy of Sveum's fourth-inning homer, it was only a side note that Nieves hadn't allowed a hit through six innings. When the Brewers broke open the game with two runs in the seventh and three more in the eighth, however, the focus shifted solely to Nieves and his quest to become the first pitcher in franchise history to throw a no-hitter.

"When it was 1–0, I was just thinking about winning the game," said Nieves. "We had a streak going. I didn't want to end that."

The small crowd was buzzing when Nieves took the mound in the bottom of the ninth. He quickly dispatched the first two hitters, getting Ken Gerhart on a ground-out and Rick Burleson on a liner to third.

When Nieves fell behind in the count, 2–0, to Ripken, Schroeder made a trip to the mound.

"Juan was like a deer in the headlights at that point," said Schroeder. "I said, 'Let's not mess this up on a 2–0 pitch. Let's put him on. We've got a 7–0 lead.' In my infinite wisdom, I decided to put Ripken on to face Eddie Murray."

Nieves obeyed orders, throwing two pitches off the plate to Ripken, walking him. When he came back with a first-pitch fastball to Murray, the future Hall of Famer sent a slicing dive to the gap in right-center. Shaded toward left for the switch-hitting Murray, who was batting from the right side, center fielder Robin Yount got on his horse. Behind the plate, Schroeder took off his mask and held his breath.

"At first, I thought it was going to be an easy out," said Schroeder. "Then, it kept slicing away. Robin was running his ass off. The harder he ran, the more the ball was slicing."

Just when it appeared the ball might fall in, spoiling Nieves's no-hit bid in heart-breaking fashion, Yount went airborne, fully

TOP 10

Top 10 Finishes in Club History

	Record	Percentage	Year
1.	95–66	.590	1979
2.	95–67	.586	1982
3.	93–69	.574	1978
4.	62–47	.569	1981*
5.	92–70	.568	1992
6.	91–71	.562	1987
7.	87–75	.537	1983
	87–75	.537	1988
9.	86–76	.531	1980
10.	83–79	.512	1991
	83–79	.512	2007

*Strike-shortened season.

stretched out, and made a spectacular catch inches above the turf. It qualified as the most sensational ending to any no-hitter in major league history, a highlight-reel gem destined to be played over and over for years to come.

"I don't know if it was the best catch I ever made, but it probably was the most memorable," conceded Yount, a former Gold Glove shortstop who moved to the outfield in 1985 after injuring his throwing shoulder.

Not only were the Brewers off to a 9–0 start, Nieves had pitched their first no-hitter. The Brewers were flying so high they almost didn't need a plane to get back to Milwaukee, but they took one anyway just to be safe. They were the talk of baseball when they opened a three-game series against Texas at electrified County Stadium, winning the first two games to stretch their streak to eleven games.

The next day was Easter Sunday, bright and crisp, as the Brewers took the field looking to make history. No American League team had begun a season with 12 consecutive victories. But, to the dismay of the 29,357 fans on hand, this apparently would be the day the magic ended. The Brewers headed into the bottom of the ninth trailing, 4–1, with seemingly little energy left. The crowd tried to change that karma by rising for a prolonged standing ovation as the players trotted back to the dugout.

"We hadn't done anything all day," said Sveum. "It looked like one of those days. But the fans got us going."

Braggs got things started by drawing a walk from erratic reliever Mitch Williams. Brock followed with a single and Cecil Cooper flied out to center. That brought to the plate the powerful Deer, who had already homered in the fifth inning. Texas manager Bobby Valentine gave Williams the hook, summoning Greg Harris for a righty versus righty matchup. Harris was a curveball pitcher, and the strikeout-prone Deer was a known sucker for breaking balls.

Sure enough, Harris started off with a curveball, which Deer missed by the proverbial country mile. Harris came back with another curve, but this time Deer didn't miss. Getting every bit of the pitch, and then some, Deer sent a drive on a mighty arc toward the left-field bleachers. Even a stiff wind blowing in from that direction couldn't contain the ball, which disappeared into the roaring crowd near the top of the stands.

"If the wind wasn't blowing in, it would have gone all the way out of the stadium," said Sveum.

Pandemonium. Deer had tied the score in Hollywood fashion, and the place was up for grabs. As he rounded first base, Deer threw up his right arm in triumph, pumping his fist. That picture would make the cover of *Sports Illustrated* later in the week.

"I don't remember running the bases," said Deer, known to his teammates as "Rooster" because of his long, flowing red mane. "I got back to the dugout and guys were jumping all over me."

Harris recovered to strike out Surhoff, but patient veteran Jim Gantner worked him for a walk on a 3–2 pitch. Up stepped the switch-hitting Sveum, batting from the left side. He, too, worked the count to 3–2, but there would be no walking this time. Sveum lit into a fast-ball from Harris and crushed it, sending a shot over the bullpen in right-center to give the Brewers a miraculous 6–4 victory.

TRIVIA

Who was the designated hitter for the Brewers on Opening Day 1987?

Answers to the trivia questions are on page 147.

*Brewers closer Dan Plesac, center, is congratulated by Mike Birkbeck, left,
and Jual Nieves after the team's 5–4 win over Chicago on April 20, 1987—a
record-tying thirteenth straight victory to start the season. The following
night the White Sox brought an abrupt end to the Brewers' streak with a 7–1
thrashing.* Photo courtesy of AP/Wide World Photos.

In the madness that followed, Sveum was summoned for two
curtain calls and yet a third with Deer in tow. Nobody wanted to go
home. Up on the loge level, where he did most of his pacing during
tense games, team president Bud Selig clapped until his hands were
numb.

To this day, all you have to say is "Easter Sunday" and Brewers
fans know exactly which game you're talking about.

"The atmosphere that day was unbelievable," said Sveum.
"When I was running the bases on my homer, I looked in the stands
and saw everybody going nuts. The ultimate thing in baseball is to

hit a walk-off home run. But that was a little bit bigger than just a walk-off homer."

The momentum carried over to the next evening in Chicago, where the Brewers rallied for a 5–4 victory over the White Sox, a nail-biter sealed by Dan Plesac's fifth save. At 13–0, the Brewers tied the major league record set by the 1982 Atlanta Braves for best start to a season. But, as they say, all good things must come to an end. The following evening at Comiskey Park, Chicago pummeled starting pitcher Mark Ciardi, who would make only one more appearance in the major leagues before later discovering his true calling as a Hollywood producer. The Brewers were never in the game, bowing 7–1 for their first loss of the season.

The Brewers bounced back to boost their record to 17–1, and were 20–3 after a 6–4 victory in Seattle on May 2. It was at that point that the Brewers lived up to their "Team Streak" nickname once again, this time in gruesome manner. They lost 12 games in a row, becoming the first team in major league history to have winning and losing streaks of at least 12 games in the same season. By the All-Star Game, the Brewers had wasted every bit of their fantastic start, hitting the break with a 42–43 record.

"When you're winning, you arrive at the ballpark saying, 'What are we going to do to win today?'" said Schroeder. "But when you're losing, you say, 'How are we going to lose this one?' We were on a roller coaster."

"Team Streak" was back at it in the second half, this time in positive fashion. Molitor took off on a club-record 39-game hitting streak, the longest in the AL since Joe DiMaggio's record of 56 games in 1941. Higuera set another club mark by pitching 32 consecutive scoreless innings. Riding those coattails, the Brewers went 49–28 in the second half to finish with a 91–71 record. It was only good enough for third place in the AL East, but the 1987

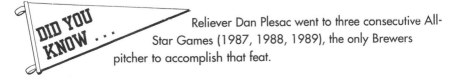

DID YOU KNOW . . . Reliever Dan Plesac went to three consecutive All-Star Games (1987, 1988, 1989), the only Brewers pitcher to accomplish that feat.

season was destined to go down as one of the most memorable in club annals.

"It's probably the greatest season a team's ever had without going to the playoffs," said Sveum. "I know that sounds kind of weird but it's true. It was as fun a season as I ever had in the major leagues. It was a phenomenal group of guys and you never knew what was going to happen next."

A Hero in Goat's Clothing

During the early years of his career, Paul Molitor couldn't stay healthy. He spent so much time in the trainer's room, he had a table reserved with his name on it. Okay, that didn't actually happen, but you get the picture.

At times, it seemed as if Molitor invented ways to get hurt. In 1980, he was voted to the starting lineup for the All-Star Game but couldn't play because of a pulled ribcage. The following season, he had surgery to repair torn ankle ligaments. After getting through the Brewers' 1982 World Series season relatively unscathed, Molitor battled through 1983 with wrist problems.

It only got worse in 1984. Molitor blew out his elbow in spring training and played only 13 games before undergoing reconstructive surgery that shelved him for the remainder of the season. Even in '85, when he won the club's comeback award, Molitor spent time on the DL with an injured ankle. The madness continued the following season when he went on the DL three separate times with hamstring strains.

Thus, it was hardly shocking in 1987 when Molitor went on the DL in May with hamstring problems, an injury that resurfaced in June. The second absence lasted three weeks and carried into the All-Star break. Normally, when a player comes off the DL, it takes some time to regain his stroke. But Molitor had a wonderfully short, uncomplicated swing that never got far out of whack. And manager Tom Trebelhorn tried to keep his best hitter's legs from breaking down again by assigning him permanently to designated hitter duty, eliminating the strain of playing defense at third base.

Molitor returned to the lineup on July 16 and went 1 for 4 with a double in a 6–4 victory over California at County Stadium. It was a modest start to the most prolific hitting spree in club history. The sweet-swinging novice DH would not go hitless again until August 26, putting together a 39-game hitting streak that captivated Brewers fans and media nationwide. It was an extraordinary offensive display, especially considering Molitor started it after coming off the DL.

Molitor had already established himself as one of the better hitters in the league. He batted .322 in 1979, his third season in the majors, and topped the .300 mark two other times. In his very first World Series game against St. Louis in 1982, he collected five hits, becoming the first player to do so in the history of the fall classic.

TRIVIA

Paul Molitor was the DH for the Brewers in the second half of the 1987 season. Who was the DH in the first half?

Answers to the trivia questions are on page 147.

But Molitor never settled into a prolonged groove such as this. In fact, few hitters in the rich annals of the game ever had. During his 39-game streak, Molitor batted a remarkable .415 with seven homers and 33 RBIs. He was uncanny in the clutch, hitting an unconscious .525 (32 for 61) with runners in scoring position. Molitor collected more than one hit 19 times during the streak, including eight three-hit games and a four-hit performance.

Beyond individual excellence, Molitor's streak had a riveting effect on the club. The Brewers staggered into the All-Star break with a 42–43 record, frittering away their record 13–0 start to the season that led to a 20–3 mark in early May. But "The Ignitor" lifted the Brewers on his shoulders and gave them one heck of a ride for the first six weeks of the second half. During Molitor's hitting streak, the Brewers went 25–15 (he sat out one game), getting their season back on track en route to a 91–71 finish—their first 90-victory season since their pennant-winning campaign in 1982.

"Paulie just carried us during that streak," said shortstop Dale Sveum. "We couldn't have been any hotter. We were the best team in baseball in the second half."

Molitor had only one of the Brewers' 11 hits on August 25 as they edged the Cleveland Indians, 10–9, in a slugfest. The next night, the

During his 39-game streak, Paul Molitor batted a remarkable .415 with seven homers and 33 RBIs. Photo courtesy of Getty Images.

TOP 10

Longest Hitting Streaks as a Brewer

	Games	Name	Year
1.	39	Paul Molitor	1987
2.	24	Dave May	1973
3.	22	Cecil Cooper	1980
	22	Corey Hart	2007
5.	19	Robin Yount	1989
	19	Paul Molitor	1989
	19	Paul Molitor	1990
	19	Darryl Hamilton	1991
	19	J. J. Hardy	2007
10.	18	Robin Yount	1980
	18	Lyle Overbay	2004

Brewers sent ace Teddy Higuera to the hill against Cleveland rookie John Farrell. Molitor's hitting streak was the talk of baseball, yet only 11,246 turned out at County Stadium to see if he could do something only four others had done in the game's history—hit safely in 40 games in a row.

Farrell, a 25-year-old right-hander, made his big-league debut eight days earlier against the Brewers in Cleveland, pitching one inning of relief. The first batter he faced was Molitor, who promptly lined a single to extend his streak to 33 games.

"I hadn't had many games during the streak where I struggled," said Molitor.

This night would be an exception. Molitor didn't have many good swings against Farrell, striking out in the first inning, grounding into a double play in the third, bouncing out to short in the sixth, and reaching on an error by Indians first baseman Pat Tabler in the eighth.

The small gathering was so focused on Molitor's at-bats that it paid scant attention to the taut pitching duel between Higuera and Farrell. It was a scoreless game through nine, which meant Molitor might get another chance in extra innings to extend his streak.

Higuera pitched into the tenth, keeping the Indians off the board with a masterful three-hitter.

Farrell yielded in the bottom of the tenth to closer Doug Jones, a change-up specialist who began his career in the Milwaukee organization and would pitch a decade later for the Brewers. Jones hit slugger Rob Deer with a pitch, and Trebelhorn sent speedy Mike "Tiny" Felder in to pinch-run. Felder moved up a base when Ernie Riles grounded out to Jones, prompting the Cleveland reliever to intentionally walk Sveum to get to hitter number nine Juan Castillo.

Trebelhorn countered with veteran outfielder Rick Manning, a left-handed hitter. With Molitor on deck, looking for a chance to keep his streak alive, it became obvious what Brewers fans wanted from Manning: an out. Jones threw a rare fastball for strike one, eliciting cheers from the stands. A stunned Manning stepped out of the batter's box to assess the bizarre situation.

"I looked down at my uniform and said, 'Is this a Cleveland uniform or a Milwaukee uniform?'" recalled Manning, who began his career with the Indians. "I knew then that they wanted me to strike out."

Manning had other ideas. He slapped the third pitch, a change-up, up the middle and the ball eluded shortstop Julio Franco, trickling into the outfield for a single. Felder scored easily with the run that gave the Brewers a 1–0 victory, but the home crowd didn't celebrate. Instead, the fans booed Manning for robbing Molitor of another chance to get a hit.

"I'm probably the only player ever to get a game-winning hit and get booed by the home fans," said Manning, who batted .228 in what would be the last of his 13 seasons in the big leagues. "That might have been one of the strangest situations ever. But the first one to get to me at first base and congratulate me was Paul. That was cool that

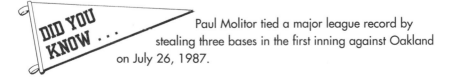

Paul Molitor tied a major league record by stealing three bases in the first inning against Oakland on July 26, 1987.

.353—Batting average by Paul Molitor in 1987, the highest in club history.

he did that. He said, 'Thank God, it's over.' He was under a lot of pressure during that streak.

"I still hear about it from people who were there that night. It never crossed my mind that I would get booed. Your goal is to win the game. I did my job. I'm sure people wanted me to make an out, then Paul could win the game with a hit and have a 40-game hitting streak. It didn't work out that way, but it was impressive to watch him do that for 39 games. Like all good things in sports, it finally came to an end. I just happened to be a part of it."

Molitor's hitting streak still stands as the fifth-longest of the 20th century, and the longest since Pete Rose set the National League record with 44 consecutive games in 1978. Rather than ponder the strange ending to the streak, Molitor reflected on the high points.

"It was pretty electric," said Molitor, who obliterated Dave May's previous club record of 24 consecutive games with a hit in 1973. "As the streak grew, every time you stepped into the box the fans would stand and cheer. It raised the hair on the back of your neck. There was a lot of pressure and media attention, with press conferences after every game, but it was all worth it. It was something special."

Out with the Old, in with the New

The Brewers responded well to manager Tom Trebelhorn, beginning with the 91–71 record of the 1987 club known as "Team Streak." Trebelhorn was an intelligent, energetic man who taught school during the off-season in Portland, Oregon. The hometown fans also responded, with more than 1.9 million going through the turnstiles of County Stadium each season from 1987 through 1989.

After an 87-victory season in '88, the Brewers slipped to 81–81 the following year and 74–88 in 1990. That slide made 1991 an important year for both Trebelhorn and his club. The season got off to a promising start when the Brewers beat future Hall of Famer Nolan Ryan on Opening Day. New second baseman Willie Randolph collected his 2,000th career hit in the home opener, and Paul Molitor became the fourth Brewer to hit for the cycle on May 15 against Minnesota.

But the season started slipping away from the Brewers as the days got warmer. A 12–15 June was followed by a horrid 9–18 July, leaving the Brewers 14 games under .500 and sinking fast in the AL East. Team president Bud Selig didn't like what he was seeing, and began to wonder if it was time to replace longtime general manager Harry Dalton.

The Brewers bounced back with a strong August (19–10), including Trebelhorn's 400th victory at the club's helm, the most by any manager in franchise history. But the die already had been cast. Selig began to put into motion plans to replace Dalton with former Brewers third baseman Sal Bando, still associated with the club as a special assistant. In turn, Bando no doubt would replace Trebelhorn, whom he thought had grown too soft with his players.

Dalton was hired to run the Brewers' baseball operation in November 1977 after serving six years in the same role with the California Angels. His arrival in Milwaukee touched off the most prosperous period in franchise history.

"One of the happiest nights of my life was when I hired Harry to be the Brewers' GM," Selig recalled. "He was with the California Angels and they hired Buzzie Bavasi [as president] and I thought Harry might be available. I called [owner] Gene Autry and asked permission to offer Harry the job. I called Harry and late that night we made a deal."

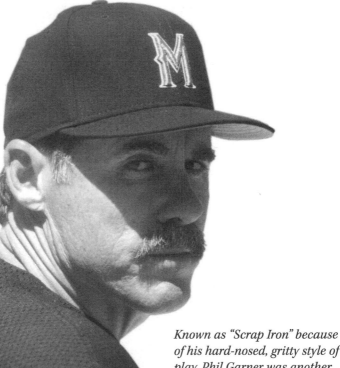

Known as "Scrap Iron" because of his hard-nosed, gritty style of play, Phil Garner was another manager that fit in well with the no-nonsense mentality of his team and its town. Photo courtesy of AP/Wide World Photos.

By the NUMBERS

13—Runs scored by the Brewers in the fifth inning on July 8, 1990, a club record for runs in an inning.

It was Dalton who made the astute personnel moves that got the Brewers to their only World Series in 1982, acquiring the likes of Pete Vuckovich, Ted Simmons, Rollie Fingers, and Don Sutton. The Brewers posted nine winning seasons under Dalton's guidance, but Selig now thought his general manager was losing his touch. Dalton's big signing of the previous off-season, first baseman Franklin Stubbs, was a colossal flop, batting a mere .213 in '91 with only 11 homers and 38 RBIs. It certainly wasn't Dalton's fault, but staff ace Teddy Higuera blew out his shoulder shortly after signing a four-year, $13.1-million contract extension. The magic of Dalton's early years in Milwaukee was all but gone.

"When Teddy got hurt, it changed everything," said second baseman Jim Gantner. "We already had lost Juan Nieves [to a shoulder injury]. Teddy was our ace. No team can lose a guy like that and not feel it. It was a big blow."

Dalton began to realize his days were numbered when Selig stopped talking to him in the final weeks of the season. Though their cramped offices were adjacent with a common doorway, Dalton began to notice that Selig went out of his way to avoid face-to-face encounters. As an indication that the die had been cast, not even a strong finish could save the jobs of Dalton and Trebelhorn. The Brewers won 10 of their final 12 games, including the last five, to finish with an 83–79 record, the third winning season in Trebelhorn's five years as manager. Going back to August, the Brewers won 40 of their last 59 games, which did nothing to alter the course that Selig had set.

TRIVIA

On May 28, 1988, a relatively unknown Brewers pitcher tossed seven and one-third innings of perfect baseball and eight and one-third innings of no-hit ball in a 2–0 victory in Cleveland. Who was he?

Answers to the trivia questions are on page 147.

THE LIST

In 1989 Brewers fans voted for the club's 20th anniversary team. The winners were:

1B	Cecil Cooper
2B	Jim Gantner
SS	Robin Yount
3B	Paul Molitor
C	Charlie Moore
OF	Sixto Lezcano
OF	Gorman Thomas
OF	Ben Oglivie
DH	Hank Aaron
RHP	Pete Vuckovich
LHP	Mike Caldwell
Closer	Rollie Fingers

Two days after the season ended, Selig informed Dalton that he was being replaced with Bando. It didn't seem to matter that the Brewers were a winning organization (1,149–1,064 record) during the years Dalton ran the show, a far cry from the underachieving campaigns prior to his arrival.

"Bud never gave me a reason," Dalton later recalled. "He said he just wanted to make a change. It was a disappointment, but I accepted it because that's baseball."

Dalton had three years remaining on his contract and remained in the organization as a senior vice president in charge of special projects before finally retiring from baseball. The game was changing, and, in Dalton's mind, not for the better.

"The objectives, the goals, were not the same," said Dalton, who passed away in 2005. "It became more of a business and less of a game."

To no one's surprise, Bando dismissed Trebelhorn the next day and launched a search for a new manager. Obviously, Trebelhorn did not agree with the decision. "They're making a mistake," he said. "I hate to leave because we didn't get done what we wanted to do, winning a championship."

It didn't take long for Bando to find Trebelhorn's replacement. Three weeks later, he tabbed Phil Garner for his first managerial role at any level. Known as "Scrap Iron" for his hard-nosed, gritty style of play, the former infielder was brought in to install the discipline and toughness that Bando thought the club lacked under Trebelhorn.

The page had been turned. The Brewers were headed in a new direction. And for one season, it appeared to be the tonic the club needed.

DID YOU KNOW . . . Paul Molitor won the fan balloting to start at second base for the AL All-Star team in 1988 despite playing in only one game at that position all season.

Off to the Races

Phil Garner played most of his 16-year major league career in the National League, a circuit in which teams manufactured runs by stealing bases, bunting runners up, and utilizing hit-and-run tactics. But the Brewers played in the American League, which featured the designated hitter and relied more on the long ball. It was no coincidence that the Brewers' golden era began with "Bambi's Bombers" and continued with "Harvey's Wallbangers."

After taking over as manager after the 1991 season, Garner took a long, hard look at the personnel on hand and decided the Brewers would get nowhere trying to out-slug opponents. They did have a healthy dose of team speed, however. Rookie shortstop Pat Listach, who unexpectedly made the club when incumbent Bill Spiers was slow to recover from back surgery, could fly. Speed also was a big part of outfielder Darryl Hamilton's game.

Even veterans such as Paul Molitor, Robin Yount, and Scott Fletcher could handle themselves on the bases. Thus, Garner decided to introduce the National League style of play to an unsuspecting AL. Soon, the Brewers would become the scourge of pitching batteries throughout the league, running and running until their tongues hung from their mouths, then running some more. No base was safe from the Brewers' special brand of thievery.

"We didn't have a home-run hitting club," said Garner. "We had to score runs doing things differently. We played a wild brand of baseball that was a lot of fun. We did a lot of things unconventionally. I did a lot of managing by my gut.

"We had guys who could run and guys who could put the ball in play. The American League wasn't used to that. They were

TOP 10

Top Individual Stolen Base Performances

	Name	Total	Year
1.	Scott Podsednik	70	2004
2.	Pat Listach	54	1992
3.	Paul Molitor	45	1987
4.	Scott Podsednik	43	2003
5.	Paul Molitor	41	1982
	Paul Molitor	41	1983
	Paul Molitor	41	1988
	Darryl Hamilton	41	1992
9.	Tommy Harper	38	1970
10.	Alex Sanchez	37	2002

playing station-to-station ball with slugging teams. We ran randomly."

When the track meet was over, the Brewers had compiled a club-record 256 stolen bases, obliterating the club record of 176 set in 1987. No other team in the AL accumulated more than 160 steals that season. Batting leadoff, Listach led the way with 54 steals—the most ever for a Brewer—en route to claiming the AL Rookie of the Year Award. Hamilton was not far behind with 41 steals.

"We forced teams to play a different style of baseball, and most of them didn't like it," said Hamilton. "American League teams were used to slugging it out and waiting for the three-run homer. We couldn't do that."

Of course, you can't win games simply by running. The Brewers also led the league in pitching (3.43 ERA) and fielding (.986 percentage), again mimicking an NL team. Another unexpected newcomer, Cal Eldred, joined the staff in the second half and proceeded to go 11–2 with a 1.79 ERA. Though Jaime Navarro led the club with 17 victories, Eldred and Chris Bosio became the hottest pitchers in the league. One day after Bosio set the club record with his 10th consecutive victory, Eldred matched that streak. No other pitcher in either league strung together that many victories.

Robin Yount and the rest of the Brewers took to the base paths under Phil Garner and gave many of their American League opponents fits with their decidedly National League style of play. Photo courtesy of Getty Images.

Preseason prognosticators were not kind to the Brewers, but their unconventional style of play kept them in the AL East race. At the All-Star break, they were 45–41, in third place and seven and one-half games back of the powerful Toronto Blue Jays. The Brewers picked up the pace a bit in August and found themselves only four and one-half games behind entering a four-game series in Toronto on the final weekend of the month.

The Brewers lost the opener to the Blue Jays in tough fashion, bowing 5–4. But they bounced back in prolific fashion the following evening. Setting club records for hits (31) and runs, the Brewers pummeled the stunned Blue Jays, 22–2, getting five runs batted in from Hamilton and Fletcher and four from Molitor. The Brewers showed the benefits of playing "small ball," with only five of their 31 hits going for extra bases.

The next day, Toronto unveiled its prized trade-deadline acquisition, right-hander David Cone. A sellout crowd of 50,413 turned out at SkyDome to watch the veteran pitcher work his magic, but Cone quickly learned that you didn't stand much chance against the Brewers without a "slide step"—the quick move to the plate designed to thwart base-stealers. The Brewers ran Cone off the field, stealing seven bases and rattling him into seven walks before he exited in the seventh inning, trailing 7–2.

TRIVIA

Pat Listach became the first Brewer to win the Rookie of the Year Award as voted on by the Baseball Writers' Association of America. Who was the AL runner-up in 1992?

Answers to the trivia questions are on page 147.

"It was so much fun," said Hamilton, who swiped a pair of bags off Cone and shell-shocked catcher Pat Borders. "You could tell that coming to the American League, it was a surprise that we were running like that. It kind of woke him up. After that, he had a slide step."

Not everyone had an appreciation for the Brewers' madcap running game, however. A few days later, in a 6–3 victory in Detroit, the Brewers stole a couple of bases in the late innings that Tigers manager Sparky Anderson thought was unprofessional. Anderson

DID YOU KNOW . . . Phil Garner finished second in balloting by the Baseball Writers' Association of America for 1992 American League Manager of the Year to Oakland's Tony La Russa.

said something about it to reporters after the game, which upset Garner.

"I don't see their big thumpers stop trying to hit home runs when they're ahead," countered Garner. "We're going to do what we've got to do. What's a safe lead against a team like that?"

The next day, the Brewers' skipper asked for a face-to-face meeting with Anderson during pregame batting practice.

"You're the grand daddy of them all and I don't want to offend you," Garner told his Hall of Fame adversary. "But this is the makeup of our club and this is what I'm going to do. I'm not trying to run it down your throat, but I don't have the power you have. You can get back in the ballgame with home runs and I can't, so I'm not shutting it down. I hope I don't offend you, but if I do, I do, and you do what you have to do."

An old-school manager, Anderson still believed the Brewers were violating the etiquette of the game. But, the following week, when the Tigers blew a couple of late-inning leads, he came around to Garner's way of thinking. "I'm not shutting down my running game anymore, either," warned Anderson, a lesson learned.

"We ruffled some feathers that year," admitted Garner. "[Tigers coach] Billy Consolo came out in the newspapers and said, 'Milwaukee's running game borders on the ridiculous.' [Brewers coach] Tim Foli came back and said, 'The difference is, when Detroit's hitters step to the plate, they're already in scoring position. We're not in scoring position until we get to third base.' That was a great line."

Team exploits took a backseat on September 9 as Yount reached a magical milestone in his Hall of Fame career with his 3,000th hit, a seventh-inning single off Cleveland's Jose Mesa. It was an electric night at County Stadium, with 47,589 packing the stands to watch the historic moment. Yount showed a true sense of drama, waiting until the final day of the homestand to reach the coveted plateau.

The Brewers blew a ninth-inning lead and lost the game to the Indians, somewhat spoiling Yount's achievement. True to his team-first nature, Yount seemed more upset about losing the game than euphoric about his individual accomplishment.

"It was nice and everything, but I really wish we would have won the game," he said afterward. "That's more important."

Earlier that day, in an owners meeting in Dallas, club president Bud Selig was named acting commissioner of baseball, an appointment that eventually would lead to him taking the job on a full-time basis. Any way you sliced it, September 9, 1992, was a watershed date in the history of the franchise.

"It's a day I'll never forget," said Selig, who got tied up in traffic heading from the airport to the ballpark and feared he would miss Yount's historic hit.

After their late-August series in Toronto, the Brewers didn't play the Blue Jays again. That turned out to be a big break for the division leaders, who lost eight of the 13 meetings with the go-go Brew Crew. Needing help from other clubs, the Brewers kept the pressure on Toronto, winning 20 of 27 games in September. By winning their first two games in October, the Brewers pulled within two games of the Blue Jays with two to play, only to be eliminated from the division race on the penultimate day when Toronto edged Detroit, 3–1. The air finally out of their balloon, the Brewers dropped their final two games in Oakland to finish their surprising season with a 92–70 record.

"Nobody expected us to do anything," said Hamilton. "We made a pretty big statement, especially for a small-market team. We gave Toronto a scare because they knew we were the only team that could consistently beat them. We ran people crazy that year. It was a lot of fun."

By the NUMBERS 11—The number of players who stole at least 10 bases for the Brewers during the 1992 season.

Into the Darkness

It didn't take long for the euphoria of the 1992 season to wear off for the Brewers. The exciting, aggressive team that surprised everyone with 92 victories was quickly dismantled as management succumbed to the economic forces that made it difficult for all small-market clubs to survive. General Manager Sal Bando was ordered to trim payroll, with disastrous results on the field.

No move was more controversial than allowing Paul Molitor to leave via free agency. Along with teammates Robin Yount and Jim Gantner, the sweet-swinging designated hitter was a cornerstone player on the club and still an offensive force. Molitor finished fourth in the AL batting race in '92 with a .320 average, socking 12 homers and driving in 89 runs while also stealing 31 bases. Known throughout his career in Milwaukee as "The Ignitor" for his role in jump-starting the offense from the leadoff spot, Molitor was the Brewers' most dynamic player by far, yet the path was paved for his exodus.

Using as his excuse that Molitor was "only a DH," Bando offered him a slight cut in his $3.4 million salary of the previous season. Many saw it as an attempt to push Molitor out the door, and he certainly was puzzled by the club's lukewarm attempts to keep him. Bando insisted the club would not offer Molitor salary arbitration, which would have extended the club's negotiating period to sign him.

The situation came to a head at the winter meetings in Louisville in December. Tipped off that Molitor was about to sign a three-year, $13-million contract with AL East rival Toronto, the Brewers offered arbitration at the eleventh hour, mostly to assure draft-pick compensation from the Blue Jays. By that point, there was no turning

TOP 10

Brewers' All-Time Home-Run Leaders

Name	Total
1. Robin Yount	251
2. Geoff Jenkins	212
3. Gorman Thomas	208
4. Cecil Cooper	201
5. Ben Oglivie	176
6. Greg Vaughn	169
7. Jeromy Burnitz	165
8. Paul Molitor	160
9. Rob Deer	137
10. Don Money	134

back for Molitor, who would have been crazy to turn down such an attractive offer from the best club in the league.

Molitor's departure created a huge firestorm among fans. Some criticized him for being disloyal and leaving the club that helped turn him into a star. But most fans leveled blasts at club president Bud Selig and Bando for playing hardball with their best player, in essence forcing him to bolt to another team.

Bando would come to regret calling Molitor "only a DH," though he later claimed that comment was taken out of context. It turned into one of the biggest public relations fiascos in club history, with more salt being rubbed into the wound when Molitor led the Blue Jays to their second consecutive World Series title in 1993, being named MVP of the Series in the process.

In succeeding years, when Molitor returned to County Stadium with Toronto, and later with his hometown Minnesota Twins, he heard his share of boos from Brewers fans still upset over his defection. Molitor characterized that response as misplaced anger, and insisted he had little choice but to leave when management made no concerted effort to keep him.

"It's the way things were going in the industry at the time, with small-market teams losing players, but it had never happened in

After the 1992 season, cost cutting forced General Manager Sal Bando to let key players go, and the Brewers sunk into oblivion with 12 consecutive losing seasons. Photo courtesy of AP/Wide World Photos.

Milwaukee," he said. "I don't think people knew how to handle it. When you look back at it now, it was just something that was kind of unavoidable."

Bando continued to defend his part in that divorce between team and star, blaming the game's changing economics that eventually led to a disastrous labor war in 1994 and the cancellation of the World Series that season.

"Maybe we should have made our best offer right out of the chute, but we couldn't match what Toronto did," insisted Bando. "The market was really changing that year and we were trying to lower our payroll."

Later, Bando admitted, "Looking back, I can't blame him one bit for anything he did."

No one ever will know how the coming years would have gone for the Brewers had Molitor stayed. The

TRIVIA

Which pitcher teamed with catcher Dave Nilsson on April 14, 1993, to form the first Australian battery in major league history?

Answers to the trivia questions are on page 147.

cost-cutting forced other important cogs on the team out the door, and the Brewers sunk into an uncompetitive mode marked by 12 consecutive losing seasons. After chasing the champion Blue Jays to the final weekend of the 1992 season, the Brewers plummeted to the bottom of the AL East in '93, finishing 26 games out of first place with a 69–93 record.

It didn't get any easier when Robin Yount, the team's competitive compass for 20 years, retired after the '93 season. One by one, the links to the team's glorious past were leaving. The Brewers stumbled into the baseball wilderness, unable to find their way. It wasn't a pretty sight for a franchise that already had gone a decade without making it to postseason play. Not even the move to the AL Central as baseball realigned in 1994 could help the Brewers compete for a division title.

"Letting Paulie go was the biggest mistake the Brewers ever made," said Gantner, who retired after the '92 season. "How could you let your best player go? You build your team around him. He made everybody else better on the team. That was devastating. I couldn't believe we let him go. He wanted to stay. When they tried, it was too late. He would have taken less years and money, with incentives, to stay. He didn't want to leave. The whole organization went down from there."

Garner's seemingly boundless optimism and enthusiasm could do nothing to change the course of a franchise that no longer had enough talent to compete. Attendance dropped almost as precipitously as the club's record, and there seemed little hope for the future.

"There was a paradigm shift in baseball," said Garner, an astute businessman off the field who understood perfectly the dynamics that made it nearly impossible for small-market teams to compete. "It became all about the money. What we were trying to do was be a family-run operation, but it was a new era. Teams with money were spending like drunken sailors.

"That started the dark years for us. If there's a criticism you can levy, it's that we probably didn't change quick enough, come up with something different. But I don't know if that's a legitimate criticism. It was what it was. We had some tough luck with injuries and other bad things happened."

If you can't afford to sign free agents, you have to develop talent from within. But the cost-cutting also compromised the Brewers' scouting department and drafting. They started drafting amateur players on the basis of "signability," bypassing those who might cost too much money. The farm system eventually fell into disarray, preventing the Brewers from returning to a competitive mode. The organization became trapped in the Bermuda Triangle of losing. The Brewers didn't have enough talent at the big-league level, they couldn't afford to buy help, and they didn't develop difference-makers from within their farm system.

"Development is a funny thing," said Garner. "You can't take Morgan horses and train them for the Kentucky Derby. You can run

By the NUMBERS

2—The number of home runs catcher Dave Nilsson hit in the sixth inning against Minnesota on May 17, 1996, becoming the first player in club history to go deep twice in the same frame.

them in the Derby, but you're not going to win. Teams like Oakland and Minnesota figured it out and developed players from within. They might have put more money into their farm system and drafting players. You've got to do what you've got to do, within your budget constraints. We just didn't have a lot of talent, so it wasn't going to work. The draft system was supposed to keep parity in the game but it became a caste system, too, because the poor teams couldn't draft players who wanted a lot of money."

Garner and his outmanned club would continue to tilt against windmills. At times, they would overachieve, considering the dearth of talent on hand. The Brewers were semicompetitive in 1996 (80–82) and 1997 (78–83), but those seasons proved to be mere blips on an otherwise discouraging radar screen. Garner would last nearly eight years as the club's manager but never would enjoy another winning season, much less repeat the magic of his rookie campaign in 1992.

Three's Company

A few days before the Brewers opened spring training in 1978, Robin Yount was riding his dirt bike on the sand dunes around Phoenix, Arizona. A daredevil by nature who loved any machine that went fast, Yount had cavorted on some type of motorized bike for as long as he could remember.

On this particular day, however, things got a bit out of hand. Yount's bike sailed off a cliff, and he was lucky to escape with only an injured foot. The promising young shortstop initially hid the injury from club officials, staying away from camp and prompting rumors to circulate that he was contemplating a career in professional golf.

"I remember the day I left camp," he said. "I'm playing short and I take one step in the hole, plant to make a throw and I fall down. I said, 'That's it. I'm out of here.'"

The truth eventually came out, with the bottom line that Yount would not be ready for the start of the season. General manager Harry Dalton and manager George Bamberger put their heads together and decided to turn shortstop over to young, untested Paul Molitor, a first-round draft pick the previous June who had only 64 minor league games under his belt at the Class A level.

That same spring, Jim Gantner made the Brewers' roster as a utility infielder. Unlike Yount and Molitor, considered can't-miss players in the big leagues, Gantner was a scrappy overachiever. The native of tiny Eden, Wisconsin, was a 12th-round draft pick in 1974 out of the University of Wisconsin-Oshkosh, a small college with a first-rate baseball program.

And thus began the long professional relationship and personal friendship of three players who became the faces of the franchise.

TOP 10

Most Career Games Played with Brewers

	Name	Total
1.	Robin Yount	2,856
2.	Paul Molitor	1,856
3.	Jim Gantner	1,801
4.	Cecil Cooper	1,490
5.	Charlie Moore	1,283
6.	Geoff Jenkins	1,234
7.	Don Money	1,196
8.	Ben Oglivie	1,149
9.	Gorman Thomas	1,102
	B.J. Surhoff	1,102

Yount, Molitor, and Gantner would go on to play 15 years together with the Brewers, the longest association of three teammates in big-league history. Molitor would move to third base when Yount returned to short, and Gantner eventually settled in at second base. They would form three-fourths of the Brewers' infield for years to come, before a shoulder injury forced Yount to move to the outfield in the mid-'80s and Molitor eventually settled into his role as a designated hitter.

Gantner, a baseball version of comedian Norm Crosby who became known for fracturing the English language, roomed with Molitor during their rookie year in the big leagues. Molitor was a young, dashing ladies man, and Gantner became accustomed to getting little sleep on the road.

"I remember all the women calling, in every town," said Gantner. "I was married but Paulie was young and single and good-looking. When you went out with him, the women would show up. They knew where he was. Sometimes, he wouldn't come back to the room until late at night. I just pretended I was sleeping. I never looked."

Though their personalities were distinctly different, Yount, Molitor, and Gantner found themselves drawn to each other. They hung out before and after games, often playing cards late into the

Jim Gantner may be the least known of the three Brewers greats who played together for 15 years, but he was more than worthy of his place alongside Paul Molitor and Robin Yount. Photo courtesy of Getty Images.

evening when the team was on the road. Their on-field competitiveness quickly transferred to the card table, where it wasn't unusual for frustrations to boil over when one or the other was losing hands.

"We played 'pluck,' hearts, spades, everything," recalled Gantner. "We played for money, not big money, but we were competitive. We'd get in disagreements. Paulie was always good for throwing the whole deck of cards. If he was losing, he'd throw the whole deck and say, 'There, we're done. End of the game.' That would be it. That happened more than once. He'd throw them right at you."

On the field, Yount and Molitor used their tremendous talents to forge Hall of Fame careers. Both had huge years in 1982, helping the Brewers claim the American League pennant and go on to their first and only World Series appearance. Gantner was a contributor as well that season, batting .295 in 132 games, but it didn't come nearly as easy on the field for the second baseman affectionately called "Gumby" by teammates and fans alike.

Gantner was a gritty, hard-nosed player who gave no quarter. He refused to bail out when turning the double play at second, an admirable approach that also cost him a pair of knee surgeries as the result of collisions with hard-sliding base runners. Fundamentally sound, Gantner was one of the best-fielding players at his position, a true pitcher's friend. Not nearly as talented as Yount or Molitor, he became a fan favorite because of his style of play, affable nature, and knack for saying and doing funny things.

TRIVIA

In 1989 Robin Yount became only the third player in major league history to win an MVP Award at two different positions (shortstop and center field). Who are the other two?

Answers to the trivia questions are on page 147.

Yount, in particular, liked to recall some of the "Gumby-isms" that kept teammates loose—such as the time Gantner showed up in spring training and announced he had gone hunting over the winter "in one of those Canadian proverbs." And the time he instructed a young infield prospect to "get up on the palms of your feet."

"He was funny without trying to be funny," said Yount. "He couldn't help himself."

Molitor, somewhat quiet and introspective by nature, never asked Yount a lot of questions about his approach to the game. Instead, he watched intently, trying to learn Yount's secret of remaining even-keeled and unflappable. Every day was a new day to Yount, who turned the page on poor outings with the best of them.

"When I got to Milwaukee, I shadowed him and watched him," said Molitor. "He's the most unselfish player I played with in 21 years. He always put team above self. He was the encourager, the guy to pat you on the back. His ability to take everything moment to moment, he did better than anybody else I've seen."

The famously unhappy Gary Sheffield, who was young and immature during his brief stint in Milwaukee from 1988–91, once suggested he didn't learn much from playing with Yount, Molitor, and Gantner. But most of their teammates cherished the lessons imparted, mostly via example on the field. One by one, the other heroes from the '82 AL champions disappeared, but the terrific trio continued to play together the only way they knew how—the right way.

"Those guys didn't have egos," said outfielder Darryl Hamilton, who broke in with the Brewers in 1988. "Two of them were Hall of Famers, but they never made you feel different on that ballclub. They set up careers for a lot of guys down the road, just with their professionalism and the way they carried themselves. I know I learned everything about playing in the big leagues from those three guys. The foundation was set because we were around three of the greatest players to ever put on a Brewers uniform."

Gantner knew he was seeing greatness on a daily basis while playing with Yount and Molitor. He was amazed at their steadiness, their penchant for doing great things in the clutch and, above all else, their humbleness and respect for the game.

"If they had played in a bigger city, they would have gotten more credit," said Gantner. "But that didn't bother them. They didn't have big egos. They never said a word. Playing alongside two future Hall of Famers, watching them play, day in and day out, that was special. You talk about leadership. Going out there every day and playing the game right, that's leadership.

"Paulie was hurt a lot early in his career. I think he would have chased 4,000 hits if he would have stayed healthy. There's no question.

By the
NUMBERS **6,399**—The combined number of hits for Robin Yount, Paul Molitor, and Jim Gantner while playing for the Brewers, a record for a trio of teammates.

He kept getting hurt in freak ways. He was in good shape; he just had bad luck. Every time he slid, we just held our breath and crossed our fingers. Moving to DH definitely helped him. If he would have stayed healthy early in his career, he would have challenged Pete Rose's hit record. I really believe that."

Yount came close to breaking up the act after the 1989 season, when his loyalty to the Brewers was tested by an unquenched desire to get back to the World Series. Feeling the team wasn't making enough progress toward that goal, Yount was tempted when the California Angels courted him as a free agent that winter. He was ready to jump ship until club president Bud Selig, with whom he had formed a uniquely tight bond, made a personal visit to Phoenix to implore him to stay in Milwaukee.

Selig, Yount, and his family gathered in the unlikely setting of a fast-food restaurant. After a prolonged discussion about the pros and cons of remaining a Brewer, Yount's wife and children departed, leaving only owner and player. There were several moments of silence before Yount spoke up.

"It would mean a lot to you if I stayed, wouldn't it?" he asked Selig.

An emotional Selig responded, "You have to understand the generation I was raised in. It was [Ted] Williams of the Red Sox and [Joe] DiMaggio of the Yankees and [Stan] Musial of the Cardinals. And they went to the Hall of Fame and it meant something. They were there, and they had played their whole career with one team. There was so much about stability and reason."

Yount listened intently, then stood up, squeezed Selig's arm, said, "Okay," and walked out the door. A relieved Selig returned to Milwaukee, euphoric that Yount would remain a Brewer.

Yount and Gantner never wore another big-league uniform during their long, successful careers. Molitor's hopes of doing likewise ended after the 1992 season when the Brewers made a half-hearted attempt to re-sign the coveted free agent, who instead

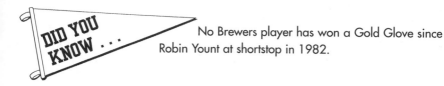

No Brewers player has won a Gold Glove since Robin Yount at shortstop in 1982.

signed a three-year deal with Toronto. Gantner also had played his last game with the Brewers, opting to retire before the '93 season. A year later, Yount made the same decision, ending his 20-year run with the Brewers.

"Splitting up was terrible," said Gantner. "It was like we were brothers."

"What was so great about having teammates like that for such a long time is that we got to know each other very well," added Molitor. "We knew what made each other tick. We were there for each other."

With free agency and escalating salaries changing the nature of the game and players jumping from team to team and league to league with frequency, it's difficult to imagine three teammates playing together for 15 seasons again.

"That was special, to play with those two guys for 15 years," said Gantner. "You'll never see that again. Not three guys. The game is different now."

Dome, Sweet Dome

During the 1990s, a tremendous building boom erupted throughout Major League Baseball, with new ballparks popping up across the country and plans put into the works for more to come. The Brewers were desperate to join the party.

Unable to generate enough revenue at aging County Stadium to keep up with escalating salaries and the runaway economics of the game, the Brewers made it clear they needed a new facility—the sooner, the better. Unfortunately, that battle took many years to win, resulting in mounting frustrations for team president and acting commissioner Bud Selig. As Selig often noted, it took considerable "pain and heartbreak" for the club's plans to finally be realized.

The major problem was this: the Brewers sought to fund a good portion of the new ballpark with a five-county sales tax that many residents, baseball fans or not, opposed. It would take passage of a financing plan by the state legislature to put such a tax in effect, and that was hardly a sure thing. Much to his dismay, Selig encountered just as many politicians opposed to the plan as those who supported it. A statewide referendum calling for the creation of a sports lottery to pay for the stadium failed miserably in April 1995, leaving it to legislators to get it done.

A stadium plan passed on October 6 of that year, but not without considerable drama. With the session of the state senate going into the wee hours of the morning, thanks to prolonged debate that didn't lack for passion, the measure finally passed by the narrowest of margins, 16–15, when George Petak of Racine switched his vote from "nay" to "yeah." Petak later would pay a tremendous price for that reversal when he was removed from office during a recall campaign

DID YOU KNOW . . . In the first Sausage Race held at Miller Park, the Bratwurst emerged from the back of the pack to nip the Italian Sausage at the wire.

in Racine. He remains the only Wisconsin legislator to be recalled, but Petak was hailed as a hero by Brewers fans fearing the club would leave town without a new facility.

"It took a lot of courage for George Petak to do what he did," said Selig. "He paid a price for it but I think most people now believe he did the right thing. Without a new ballpark, the Brewers had no chance to survive in Milwaukee. That became quite evident."

In March 1996, the Miller Brewing Company announced it would pay $41.2 million over 20 years for naming rights to the retractable-roof facility, now known as Miller Park. To the dismay of those who wanted the new ballpark downtown, it would be built adjacent to County Stadium, a few miles away. There was a ceremonial ground-breaking in November of that year, with a target date of opening for the start of the 2000 season.

Those plans had to be pushed back a year after a horrible accident at the construction site on July 14, 1999. A 467-foot crane dubbed "Big Blue" collapsed while lifting a 450-ton steel piece of the roof infrastructure, killing three ironworkers, Jeffrey Wischer, William DeGrave, and Jerome Starr, and causing immense damage to the stadium, later estimated at $100 million. It was a tragic day that Selig will never forget.

TRIVIA

Who collected the first hit in Miller Park?

Answers to the trivia questions are on page 147.

Selig was in the commissioner's office in downtown Milwaukee that afternoon when his daughter, Brewers president Wendy Selig-Prieb, called with news of the crane collapse. Selig had just returned from the All-Star Game in Boston, an uplifting three days that included a moving tribute to legendary Ted Williams at Fenway Park.

"You better turn on your TV," Selig's daughter said solemnly.

Selig did so and couldn't believe his eyes. Television helicopters gave aerial views of the vast devastation at the construction site, a horrific picture that was difficult to comprehend. Selig sat transfixed, tears streaming down his face.

"It was the beginning of a very sad evening," he recalled. "Very sad."

Selig went to the construction site that evening, meeting with his daughter and city officials, who gathered to survey the damage. There were hugs and tears as everyone tried to comprehend the magnitude of the tragedy and what might lie ahead.

The next evening, Selig took part in one of the most bittersweet events of his commissionership. He traveled to Seattle for the opening of the Mariners' new retractable-roof ballpark, Safeco Field, where joyous fans turned out to celebrate. But Selig's heart was back in Milwaukee.

The retractable roof was open at Miller Park as the MLB All-Star Game got under way on July 9, 2002, in the Brewers' spectacular new stadium. Photo courtesy of AP/Wide World Photos.

"I don't mind telling everybody that it's as painful an experience as I've ever gone through, a very sad and emotional experience," Selig said at a press conference that night, tears welling in his eyes. "I thought about not coming here, but obviously the Milwaukee team is in very good hands."

Life goes on, and the Brewers and construction officials regrouped. The rubble was removed, the damage repaired, proper tributes were made to the fallen ironworkers, and the project resumed. The opening of Miller Park was pushed back to the beginning of the 2001 season. After years of frustration in getting the funding put together, the divisiveness created by the project and the immense sadness of lives lost and the destruction of the crane collapse, April 6, 2001, was finally a day to celebrate. The Brewers

Fun Facts About Miller Park

- The roof weighs 12,000 tons and covers 10.5 acres.
- The 1.2 million-square-foot ballpark sits on a 265-acre site. Miller Park weighs 500,000 tons, the equivalent of 62.5 million 16-pound bowling balls.
- More than 2.2 million hours of construction work were expended on building the ballpark.
- There are 338,000 concrete masonry blocks in the ballpark, enough to enclose a 30-story building.
- The ballpark contains 72,000 cubic yards of concrete, enough to pave a four-foot-wide sidewalk for 10 miles.
- The height of Miller Park is nearly 300 feet, roughly twice that of County Stadium. Inside, the roof peaks about 200 feet above second base.
- The outfield dimensions were designed with ideas from Hall of Fame outfielder Robin Yount and general manager Sal Bando.
- The roof is designed to withstand snow drift loads of 170 pounds per square foot, or about 12 feet of snow.
- The ballpark contains 66 restrooms: 33 for men and 33 for women.
- Total elapsed construction time, through April 6, 2001 (including repair time for the July 14, 1999, crane accident that caused $100 million in damage): 53 months.
- Fans seated in the first row of seats behind home plate at Miller Park will be closer to the catcher than the pitcher is. The pitching rubber is 60 feet, six inches from home plate. The first row of seats is 56 feet from the plate.

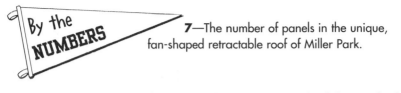

opened their magnificent new home, a watershed day in the history of the franchise. County Stadium, which had served the Milwaukee Braves and Brewers so well over the years, had been razed. Wisconsin's weather, as fickle a dancer partner as a team could have, no longer was a factor in the playing of Major League Baseball in the city. The roof was closed for the opener, keeping out the 43-degree chill.

In so many ways, it was a new day.

"Well, we're home," shortstop Mark Loretta announced during pregame ceremonies, in succinct yet appropriate remarks.

As might be expected, Selig was emotional during his opening remarks. Wearing a white Major League Baseball jacket, Selig told the audience, "It's hard for me to articulate, for one of the few times in my life, how I feel today."

With flashbulbs popping throughout the stands, President George W. Bush and Selig took turns making ceremonial first pitches. A sold-out, enthusiastic audience of 42,024 then settled in to watch the Brewers christen their new ballpark with a dramatic 5–4 victory over the Cincinnati Reds, courtesy of Rich Sexson's tape-measure home run in the bottom of the eighth. It was a chilly, rainy night in what passes for spring in Wisconsin but no one noticed with the facility's signature fan-shaped roof closed.

"You really couldn't write a better script," Brewers manager Davey Lopes said afterward, summing up both the game and the advent of the Miller Park era.

If at First You Don't Succeed

The feistiness and hard-nosed approach that Phil Garner displayed as a player led to his nickname "Scrap Iron." Garner brought that same fiery attitude to his job as the Brewers' manager.

Garner once found himself in a face-to-face confrontation with Oakland manager Tony La Russa at home plate, resulting in a wild, bench-clearing brawl between the teams. On another occasion, Garner publicly challenged White Sox broadcasters Ken "Hawk" Harrelson and Tom Paciorek to a fight when they suggested on the air that Chicago pitchers should retaliate for what they considered the intentional plunking of hitters by the Brewers' staff.

Garner wasn't afraid to get in the face of his players, either. During the 1992 season, he got into a screaming match on the mound with right-hander Chris Bosio, whose tempestuous nature helped spark the conflagration.

"I'm ready to fight and he's ready to fight," said Garner, who was upset when Bosio hit a batter that he didn't want to pitch to, setting up a big rally by the Yankees. "He's jawing with the guy on base and I say, 'Boz,' and he turns around and says, 'What the hell do you want?' I take him out of the game and tell him to go to my office and wait until the end of the ballgame."

After the game, Garner stormed into the manager's office, slammed the door shut, and proceeded to go face-to-face with Bosio for 30 minutes. Neither backed down but Garner eventually called a truce when his voice cracked under the strain.

"I got so tired of yelling, I said, 'Boz, I'm exhausted,'" recalled Garner. "We talked it out and from that point, he went out and won 10 straight ballgames. I never had another problem with Boz."

TOP 10

Single-Season Pitching Strikeout Leaders

	Name	Total	Year
1.	Ben Sheets	264	2004
2.	Teddy Higuera	240	1987
3.	Doug Davis	208	2005
4.	Teddy Higuera	207	1986
5.	Teddy Higuera	192	1988
6.	Cal Eldred	180	1993
7.	Chris Capuano	176	2005
8.	Chris Capuano	174	2006
9.	Chris Bosio	173	1989
10.	Ben Sheets	170	2002

That same year, Garner became flustered with Bill Wegman, a God-fearing, hardworking pitcher who just didn't have it in him to intentionally throw at hitters. Toronto's Joe Carter was wearing out Wegman that season, and Garner couldn't figure out why the tall right-hander wouldn't knock the slugger off the plate with a brush-back pitch or two.

"I said, 'Weggie, it's entirely appropriate when a guy's beating you like this guy to throw the ball in on him, and if you hit him in the butt, you hit him in the butt,'" recalled Garner. "He said, 'I can't do it. That's against my religion.' I said, 'God's got nothing to do with it. This is between you and Joe Carter, and right now, he's killing you.' But he was dead serious, so in the last few weeks of the season, I had to take him out of the game if Carter came up in a key situation.

"The next year, we were playing the White Sox and Ron Karkovice was having a big day against Weggie. The next time he came up, the first pitch was inside and the next pitch was inside. I said to [pitching coach] Don Rowe, 'Don, I think he's trying to hit him.' So, apparently, his religious beliefs changed when he kept getting beat around."

Garner's give-no-quarter attitude made him a favorite of his players, Brewers fans, the media, and his boss, general manager Sal

Bando. But losing has a way of pushing one's positive attributes into the background, and the outclassed Brewers had suffered through six consecutive losing seasons under Garner when the 1999 campaign began. The team was still playing hard, and it appeared Garner would survive when the Brewers hovered near the .500 mark in late July. But the roof started to cave in during the early days of August, and a six-game losing streak took some of the fight out of the club. Bando began to think it was time for a change, whether it was Garner's fault or not.

Commissioner Bud Selig introduces Mark Attanasio as the new owner of the Milwaukee Brewers during a news conference on January 13, 2005. Team owners unanimously approved the $223-million sale of the Brewers by Selig's family to an investment group headed by Attanasio. Photo courtesy of AP/Wide World Photos.

On August 12, Bando announced he was firing Garner and replacing him on an interim basis with hitting coach Jim Lefebvre. Bando then stunned many by also stepping down, saying he had come in as a package deal with his manager and felt it was best if they left together. Bando was reassigned within the organization, which was now being run by Wendy Selig-Prieb, daughter of former Brewers president Bud Selig, who surrendered control when he became commissioner of baseball on a full-time basis in 1998.

TRIVIA

Which team declined to move from the American League to the National League in 1998, paving the way for the Brewers to make the switch?

Answers to the trivia questions are on page 147.

There had been hopes that moving the Brewers to the National League in '98 would re-energize the organization. Milwaukee fans still upset over the exodus of the Braves to Atlanta in 1966 were pleased to see the city return to its NL roots, but the change did not prove to be a panacea. The team went 74–88 and finished fifth in the NL Central, a whopping 28 games out of first place.

With the Brewers now missing both general manager and manager, the search began for new leadership for the organization. Dean Taylor, an assistant to longtime Atlanta general manager John Schuerholz, was tapped to run the baseball operation. He, in turn, named Davey Lopes as manager, putting an African American in that role for the first time in club history.

As usual, Taylor and Lopes said all the right things about turning around a team that had suffered seven consecutive losing seasons.

"I'm asking each member of this organization to do one thing," Taylor said at his introductory press conference. "To challenge himself or herself when they come through the door every day to work for the Milwaukee Brewers—whether they are walking through the doors of the office or they are walking through the doors of the clubhouse—they need to walk through that door with the expectation that they are going to win."

Lopes, an intense, no-nonsense taskmaster hired to whip the team into shape, promised, "I can guarantee you are going to see a

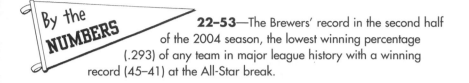

22–53—The Brewers' record in the second half of the 2004 season, the lowest winning percentage (.293) of any team in major league history with a winning record (45–41) at the All-Star break.

club that is very energetic, hardworking, and will put on a good show for the fans."

Those promises went unfulfilled, however, and the losing continued. The Brewers won 73 games in 2000, one less than the previous year. Even the opening of Miller Park in 2001, which allowed the club to significantly expand its payroll, could not get the Brewers headed in the right direction. After winning only 68 games that season, Lopes's job was squarely on the line as the 2002 season began. What followed was the biggest debacle in franchise history.

Put in jeopardy by questionable personnel moves by those above him, such as the signing of injury-prone free agent outfielder Jeffrey Hammonds, Lopes never really had a chance. The Brewers staggered to a 3–12 start, worst in franchise history, and after a mere 15 games, Lopes was dismissed. Calling it a "very, very difficult decision," Taylor replaced him on an interim basis with Coach Jerry Royster, who ironically had been Lopes's closest confidant.

If Taylor hoped the quick-trigger move would awaken his ballclub, he was badly mistaken. The overmatched Brewers went on to lose 106 games, completing the franchise's worst season. There were countless embarrassing moments, such as the May 23 game against Los Angeles in which Shawn Green belted four home runs, setting a major league record by accumulating 19 total bases. Lopsided defeats became the order of the day, and it didn't help when outfielder Geoff Jenkins was lost on June 17 with a horribly dislocated ankle. Signaling a total breakdown in discipline, there were clubhouse fights as well as a memorable confrontation on the mound between Royster and reliever Mike DeJean.

It was a doomed season in many ways at Miller Park. The Brewers hosted the All-Star Game for the first time since 1975, but the managers ran out of players and the game ended in a 7–7 tie, a huge embarrassment for Selig in the ballpark of the club he once ran.

By the end of the season, it became apparent that another major shakeup at the top of the Brewers hierarchy was inevitable.

And what a shakeup it was. Taylor was replaced with Doug Melvin, a former general manager with the Texas Rangers. Melvin later named as his manager Ned Yost, who played for the Brewers in their glory days in the early '80s. Selig-Prieb stepped down as club president, naming local attorney Ulice Payne Jr. as her successor (Payne, in turn, would last only one season on the job, leaving in a dispute with the board of directors over the team's payroll budget).

There would be more changes to come. In January 2004, it was announced that the Brewers were for sale. Los Angeles investor Mark Attanasio was confirmed as the club's new owner a year later, ending 35 years of ownership and operation by the Selig family. On and off the field, it was a franchise in transition. It's a long road back when you've hit rock bottom, and the Brewers won only 68 and 67 games in the first two years under Yost.

The Brewers' 12-year losing streak finally came to an end in 2005, although just barely. When they took the field for a season-ending, three-game series in Pittsburgh, the Brewers needed one victory to assure a break-even season and an end to the madness. Wisconsin native Damian Miller led the way with a two-run seventh-inning homer, giving the Brewers a come-from-behind 6–5 victory over the Pirates.

"As I was running down the first-base line, I heard everybody yelling in the dugout, like we had just won the seventh game of the World Series," said Miller. "It was a great feeling."

A chance for a winning season slipped away when the Brewers, out of gas after pushing so hard through September, dropped the final two games to the Pirates. But an 81–81 finish never felt so good.

DID YOU KNOW . . . The interlocking "ball and glove" logo the Brewers used from 1978 through 1993 (which was resurrected on "retro" uniforms in 2006) was designed by Tom Meindel, an art history student at the University of Wisconsin–Eau Claire. Meindel won a contest with more than 2,000 entries in a month-long contest in October and November of '77.

"We're through with 12 years of losing," said Yost, who helped return the Brewers to a competitive mode after being a laughing-stock for so long. "Nobody can call us losers anymore."

Injuries derailed the Brewers in 2006, resulting in a step back-ward and a 75–87 finish. But, at long last, there was light at the end of what had been a very long and dark tunnel. The Brewers no longer were a club to take lightly. They had emerged from the baseball wilderness, with hopes of better days ahead.

The Big Tease

When the Brewers broke training camp in the spring of 2007, there was good reason for a level of optimism that had not been associated with the club for many years.

For starters, there was the 25-year itch thing. In 1957 the Milwaukee Braves overcame their undeserved "Bushville" moniker to knock off the mighty New York Yankees and win the World Series. Twenty-five years later, the '82 Brewers came within a victory of repeating that feat.

Were the baseball gods scheduled to shine on Milwaukee every 25 years?

"I don't know if I believe in it, but it sure sounds good," manager Ned Yost said before the club headed north. "Every 25 years works for me."

Injuries played a large role in derailing the hopes of the 2006 Brewers, who failed to build on the momentum of an 81–81 season the previous year. But the additions of veteran right-hander Jeff Suppan and catcher Johnny Estrada, as well as versatile infielder and Milwaukee native Craig Counsell, to a strong nucleus of young players resulted in a deep club that many picked as the dark-horse candidate in the National League Central.

The improved talent level would be tested immediately in a tough April schedule that began with a homestand against the Dodgers and the Cubs, not to mention 14 games on the road, where the Brewers played miserably in '06 (27–54).

Counsell proved to be a sage when he stressed the importance of getting off to a solid start to build the team's confidence, particularly among the talented group of young players including first baseman

Prince Fielder, shortstop J.J. Hardy, outfielder Corey Hart, and second baseman Rickie Weeks.

"I do think we have to prove it to ourselves," said Counsell, who knows exactly what it takes to win after picking up World Series rings with Florida in 1997 and Arizona in 2001. "We've got to get to the point where we believe we're a good team. I think that has to happen early in the season for us.

"We haven't been to the playoffs in a long, long time. Good teams have that real belief that they're going to win."

Given that mandate, the Brewers bolted to the fastest start in club history. Concluding a sensational 9–1 homestand with a 3–1 victory over Washington on May 9, the Brewers held a stunning 24–10 record, the best in the major leagues. Suddenly, a team that hadn't had a winning season since 1992 was the darling of the baseball world.

Fielder and Hardy led the way offensively, socking 10 and nine home runs, respectively. Left-hander Chris Capuano went 5–0 in his first seven starts and closer Francisco Cordero racked up a major league–best 15 saves in those first 24 victories.

Already evolving as the clubhouse leader at the tender age of 23, Fielder attributed the team's fast start to a noticeable change in attitude. Players no longer hoped for the best and expected the worst. A quiet confidence was building day by day in a group of players that already knew they were good enough to win the division.

"Instead of hoping to make things happen, we expect it now," said Fielder. "We go out and play hard every day. If we win, that's over. And if we lose, that's over, too. In baseball, you have to stay focused on the day-to-day stuff. If we keep playing like this, I think we have a shot."

Veteran left fielder Geoff Jenkins, who has experienced mostly misery since coming to the big leagues with the Brewers in 1998, was almost giddy over the team's early success.

"In the past, we've had some just horrible teams," said Jenkins. "You come to the ballpark, and it's July, and you're already out of the race."

Asked to assess his club's performance to date, Yost merely said, "It can't go any better. You just ride it out. It's a long year."

TOP FIVE

National League Rookie Home-Run Leaders

With 34 home runs in 2007, Ryan Braun posted the fifth-highest home-run total by a rookie in National League history. Here's a look at the top five players to have achieved the same feat.

	Name	Team	Year	HR
1.	Wally Berger	Boston	1930	38
	Frank Robinson	Cincinnati	1956	38
3.	Albert Pujols	St. Louis	2001	37
4.	Mike Piazza	Los Angeles	1993	35
5.	Ryan Braun	Milwaukee	2007	34

Yost had no way of knowing at the time just how bumpy that ride would become in the coming weeks.

Things began to turn sour during a 2–5 trip to New York and Philadelphia. The Brewers returned home briefly to lose two of three to Minnesota in an interleague series, then continued to fall apart on a disastrous 1–5 West Coast trip to Los Angeles and San Diego.

The opposition got considerably tougher during that stretch and the now-listing Brewers didn't seem up to it. With the offense in a general malaise, general manager Doug Melvin made a move that would pay off in stunning fashion down the road, summoning third baseman Ryan Braun from Class AAA Nashville.

With Corey Koskie still sidelined with post-concussion syndrome from the previous season, the Brewers began the year with veterans Tony Graffanino and Counsell platooning at third base. Neither could get going at the plate, however, prompting the call for Braun, a 2005 first-round draft pick considered an offensive prodigy who needed some work to get up to speed on the field.

The Brewers "infield of the future" suddenly became their "infield of the present." Fielder (2002), Weeks (2003), and Braun had all been first-round picks, and Hardy (2001) was a second-rounder. During their losing years leading into and out of the new millennium, the Brewers had drafted wisely, stockpiling a wealth of talent

Brewers first baseman Prince Fielder watches his two-run home run—one of 50 he hit in 2007 to lead the NL—leave the park during the eighth inning of the August 4 game against the Phillies. Photo courtesy AP/Wide World Photos

in the minor league system that would help turn around the club's fortunes.

Some questioned whether a team could win with such a young infield, but it was the Brewers' plan all along to build from within the system and add veteran players from outside when appropriate. Yost gave a nod to scouting director Jack Zduriencik, farm director Reid Nichols, and their staffs. "Not near enough credit goes to our scouting and player development people," Yost said. "It's a pretty nice core group of four players right there. They're given the opportunity to become better players. The ones that do are the ones who get here."

The Brewers put a temporary halt to their skid with a 5–5 homestand against Atlanta, Florida, and Chicago, but proceeded to lose two of three in Texas. Then, on June 12 in Detroit, they hit rock bottom in many ways. Completely overmatched by hard-throwing Tigers right-hander Justin Verlander, the Brewers were no-hit for the third time in club history, losing for the 20th time in 30 games.

The team's 24–10 start suddenly seemed like eons ago. Now 34–30 and taking on that deer-in-the-headlights look, the Brewers showed no signs of gaining a foothold. Their season suddenly hung in the balance, and nervous fans wondered if their once-promising team would bottom out completely.

Yost refused to blame the slide on playing tougher competition, despite the Brewers 18–10 record against obviously weak National League Central foes and 16–20 mark outside the division. "You can't ever get me to admit that," he insisted. "I don't see that."

With the Brewers in desperate need of something—anything—positive, Bill Hall produced the biggest at-bat of the season the following night at Comerica Park. Behind 2–1 to the Tigers, the Brewers were four outs away from yet another loss when Hall crushed a two-run homer, his first in nearly a month, off reliever Fernando Rodney to pave the way for a heart-pounding 3–2 victory. Just as important was the performance of young right-hander Carlos Villanueva, who came out of the bullpen to replace Capuano when he suffered a groin injury while warming up. "It was a full team win," said Yost. "We had to scratch and claw, with just about the whole team."

And just like that, the Brewers suddenly got hot again. They won 12 of their next 14 games to move back to 14 games over .500, and all was right in their world.

One of the highlights of that resurgence came on June 17 in Minnesota, and believe it or not, it didn't take place in a victory. Coming from seven runs down after five innings, the Brewers roared back to tie the Twins, 9–9, only to lose in heartbreaking fashion on Justin Morneau's home run in the bottom of the ninth. But the talk afterward on the flight home was not about the comeback efforts or the walk-off defeat. What had the Brewers buzzing was the unlikeliest inside-the-park home run of the major league season.

Leading off the top of the ninth, Fielder hit a towering fly to straightaway center. As happens to many fielders during day games at the Metrodome, Twins center fielder Lew Ford lost the ball in the backdrop of the white fabric roof, and it landed a good 25 yards away from where he stopped, arms in the air.

"Halfway to first, I saw he didn't see it," said Fielder. "I just started running."

And running and running. When the 262-pound slugger got to third base and saw coach Nick Leyva waving him home, Fielder's eyes got big. He did a few chop steps at the bag and emptied his gas tank. He scored standing up with such a head of steam that he was unable to slow down before roaring into the visiting dugout, where he was swarmed by laughing, smiling teammates.

"It was like I was back in Little League," said Fielder, who recalled that his last inside-the-parker was at that level because "the kids couldn't really throw the ball back in."

The Brewers slipped again entering the break, losing seven of their final 10 games to bring their record to 49–39. The All-Star Game in San Francisco proved to be a festive occasion for the club, which sent four representatives to the contest for the first time since 1983. Fielder became the first Brewer to be voted to the starting lineup by the fans since Paul Molitor in 1988, and he was joined on the National League club by Hardy, Cordero, and staff ace Ben Sheets.

"This is unbelievable," said Cordero. "At the beginning of the year, nobody was talking about the Brewers."

"I love it," said Yost, whose club led the National League Central by four and a half games. "It makes my year. This is like being knighted. When you get elected to the All-Star team, you get a title that stays with you forever."

One of the keys to the Brewers' feel-good first half was the return to health of Sheets, who had been hampered by various shoulder issues since August 2005. Sheets won 10 games before the break, beginning with a two-hitter on Opening Day against Los Angeles. But a red flag went up on the Brewers' playoff hopes just two games into the second half when Sheets suffered an injury to the middle finger of his pitching hand in a start against Colorado. It would be six weeks before he returned to the mound, and the Brewers slipped into a prolonged funk in his absence.

There was no way of knowing that Sheets's injury would be compounded by the extended droughts suffered by two other starters, Capuano and Suppan. Capuano would pitch in 16 consecutive team losses before finally being removed from the rotation, his 5–0 beginning a distant memory. Suppan would go through 12 starts without a victory, though unlike Capuano, the Brewers didn't lose every one of those games.

An 11–16 record for July was followed by a disastrous 9–18 for August as the Brewers gave back the first-place cushion they had worked so hard to build. After leading the division for 102 consecutive days, the Brewers fell percentage points behind the Cubs with an 8–5 loss to the New York Mets on August 1. Tensions built, and the next day Yost was caught on camera in a dugout altercation with Graffanino and Estrada during an ugly 12–4 loss to the Mets. Six days later, Graffanino was lost for the season with a knee injury during a hideous 19–4 pummeling in Colorado.

With the team seemingly helpless to pull out of its freefall, the unthinkable happened on August 28 in Chicago. With their fifth consecutive defeat, the Brewers actually fell a game below .500 at 65–66. They had gone an unfathomable 17–32 since the All-Star break; they had been 14 games above .500 just six days before it. Suddenly people started asking if a team with so many young players was up to the challenge of its first pennant race in 15 years.

"Realistically, we have played .500 baseball once in 15 years [in 2005], and now we're focusing on winning a championship," said Yost. "That's a big jump, with a lot of expectations. These kids are in uncharted territory for them, this time of year.

"You have to learn to embrace that and accept that and produce. They deeply desire to play well and win. They want to win this with every fiber they have. There's not one out there that doesn't."

The return of Sheets from the disabled list the next day seemed to re-energize the Brewers. He beat the Cubs in his first game back and the team started to win again. The two youngest pitchers on the team, Yovani Gallardo, 21, and Villanueva, 23, became fixtures in the starting rotation and stabilized what had been a shaky area.

The Brewers moved back on top of the Cubs for a brief period in early September as the teams jockeyed back and forth for the playoff spot. After routing Houston 9–1 at Minute Maid Park on September 18 for their fourth consecutive victory, the Brewers found themselves percentage points ahead of Chicago with 12 games to go.

By the NUMBERS

231—The number of home runs slugged by the Brewers in 2007, a record that led the major leagues and shattered the franchise record of 216 established by "Harvey's Wallbangers" in 1982.

But the Brewers had been unable to string together victories on the road all season, and that puzzling trend would hurt them again, this time badly. After losing the last game in Houston, the Brewers went to Atlanta and dropped three of four during a frustrating weekend in which Cordero blew a save with one out to go and Yost and his players accused the umpires of being the difference by blowing calls in another loss.

In a span of five days the Brewers slipped from a virtual tie for first to three and a half games behind the Cubs. With only seven days remaining in the season, it would prove to be a deficit too large to overcome. The Brewers were eliminated from the division race with two games remaining on the schedule, bowing to San Diego at home while the Cubs pummeled an injury-depleted Cincinnati club.

With an 81–79 record, the Brewers had to split their remaining games against the pitching-rich Padres—fighting for a playoff berth—merely to assure their first winning campaign since 1992. For some franchises that wouldn't sound like a lofty goal, but the Brewers were determined to field a winner, coming from behind twice against San Diego to finish at 83–79.

TRIVIA

In 2007 first baseman Prince Fielder became the youngest player (23 years, 139 days) to hit 50 home runs in a season. Who held the record previously?

Answers to the trivia questions are on page 147.

Yes, there was general dismay over not winning a division the team had led for most of the season, but the Brewers firmly believed they were headed in the right direction for next year.

"There's no doubt it's a disappointment. We're all disappointed," said Yost. "But, to think we gave it away or let it slip away, that wasn't the case. We gave it our best effort. It didn't work out. Next year we come back better, we come back more experienced.

"For anybody to think this year was a failure or that we didn't accomplish anything, they're dead wrong. It's a step-by-step process. There's nothing left for us to accomplish next year except winning the division."

For once, "wait 'til next year" didn't sound like a hollow cry.

This Bud's for You

Some of Bud Selig's fondest memories hark back to his youth, when his mother would take him to Borchert Field in Milwaukee to watch the minor league Brewers play. The impressionable youngster had no way of knowing at the time that he would grow up to be the owner of the major league Brewers one day.

Selig's passion for the game created that particular destiny and, later, a much larger role in the sport. Not only would he go on to operate the Brewers for more than 30 years, he would become commissioner of baseball, on an interim basis at first, then full time, overseeing both turbulent times and an era of great growth in the game.

No Milwaukeean was more ecstatic than Selig when the Braves moved to the city from Boston in 1953. He loved going to County Stadium to watch Hank Aaron and Eddie Mathews and Warren Spahn, not to mention the litany of legendary stars who wore the uniforms of the enemy. Selig attended the Braves' very first game, making the two-hour drive from Madison, where he was a sophomore at the University of Wisconsin.

"When Billy Bruton hit the home run off [St. Louis outfielder] Enos Slaughter's glove to win the game, it was just wild," he recalled. "It became a love affair with the intensity that no one could have predicted."

On the flip side, no one was more dismayed when the Braves bolted for Atlanta after the 1965 season. Selig formed Teams, Inc., a group that unsuccessfully sued to keep the team in Milwaukee. The lame-duck club alienated its fan base, and only 12,577 showed up for the final game at County Stadium on September 22, 1965. Selig was

141

one of them, and stood with tears in his eyes as the home team trudged off the field for the final time after an extra-inning loss to the Dodgers.

"Somebody tapped me on the back and I turned around, and this older woman was standing there," recalled Selig. "She said, 'You're all we've got now. Don't let us down.'"

Selig didn't let down the baseball fans of the city. It took a few years of dogged pursuit, with many frustrating days mixed in, but Selig finally returned Major League Baseball to Milwaukee when his

Though Bud Selig's passion for baseball has led him beyond Milwaukee, his love for the Brewers and his role in their history will always be among his proudest accomplishments. Photo courtesy of AP/Wide World Photos.

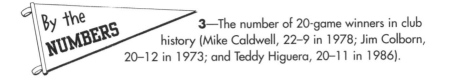

By the NUMBERS

3—The number of 20-game winners in club history (Mike Caldwell, 22–9 in 1978; Jim Colborn, 20–12 in 1973; and Teddy Higuera, 20–11 in 1986).

group purchased the Seattle Pilots out of bankruptcy and renamed them the Brewers.

"It was probably the toughest five years of my life in terms of frustration and disappointment," he said. "But it was a great teacher for me, too. It taught me to be tenacious and have patience.

"Of all the marvelous things that have happened to me, including becoming commissioner of baseball, bringing baseball back to Milwaukee will always be my proudest accomplishment because the odds were stacked against us tremendously."

True to his initial status as a fan, Selig lived and died with his franchise over the years. When times were good, such as the 1982 World Series season, he could be found out on the outdoor loge level, clapping and cheering with the rest of the crowd. During tough times, and there were many, he would stomp through the press box, muttering curse words and slamming the door to the owner's box behind him. Tom Skibosh, who spent 19 years as the club's media relations director, later wrote a book titled *If You Wanna Have Fun, Go Someplace Else!*—a direct admonishment from Selig one night when Skibosh and assistant Mario Ziino were not acting solemn enough in the owner's eyes during a poor performance by the Brewers.

While operating the Brewers, Selig found enough spare time to take an active role in the management of the game. He served tirelessly on ownership committees when others had no interest, and, little by little, his influence spread. "Get Buddy to do it" became a common cry among his peers when thankless, tedious tasks needed to be performed. No owner was more distraught than Selig on September 1, 1989, the day Commissioner Bart Giamatti died of a heart attack after only five months on the job.

"I really believe Bart would have been a great commissioner," said Selig. "He was such a smart man, and he really loved the game. That was such a sad day."

TOP 10

Most Saves in a Season

	Saves	Name	Year
1.	40	Francisco Cordero	2007
2.	39	Derrick Turnbow	2005
	39	Dan Kolb	2004
4.	37	Bob Wickman	1999
5.	36	Doug Jones	1997
6.	33	Dan Plesac	1989
7.	32	Mike Fetters	1996
8.	31	Ken Sanders	1971
9.	30	Dan Plesac	1988
10.	29	Rollie Fingers	1982
	29	Doug Henry	1992

Selig and other owners were not nearly as enamored with Giamatti's successor, Fay Vincent, whom they felt catered more to the players union than management. With Selig and Chicago White Sox owner Jerry Reinsdorf playing key roles, Vincent was ousted from office on Labor Day weekend of 1992. A few days later, Selig was named by his peers as acting commissioner, with the official title of executive council chairman. True to his real love—the game itself—Selig rushed back from that September 9 meeting in Texas to watch Brewers Hall of Famer Robin Yount collect his 3,000[th] hit that evening.

Over the six years Selig served as acting commissioner, he found less and less time to devote to the Brewers. He gradually shifted control of the daily operation of the club to his daughter, Wendy Selig-Prieb, who became the Brewers' president. That shift became permanent on July 9, 1998, when Selig was named commissioner on a full-time basis. He transferred his ownership interest in the Brewers to his daughter to remove any conflict of interest, though many refused to believe he no longer kept his hand in the club's business matters.

"My focus changed completely," Selig insisted.

But not before he secured the future of the Brewers in Milwaukee by spearheading efforts to build Miller Park, which opened in 2001 and halted any fears that the club would move to a bigger market. Everyone involved in that project, friend or foe, agreed that the new ballpark never would have happened if not for Selig's tireless efforts and absolute refusal to take no for an answer. Yet, as ugly as that battle became, he never publicly threatened to move the Brewers to another city.

"That would not have been the right thing to do," said Selig. "You don't get things done by making threats. I knew how important the Brewers were to the city. It was important to find a way that allowed the team to stay in Milwaukee."

It was Selig's ability to cajole, persuade, plead, and generally beat down opposition that made him a natural for the commissioner's job. His talent for building consensus on issues finally bonded owners and helped get economic concessions from the players union, which had dominated the labor wars for years. The early days were tough, especially when Selig had to step to a microphone in September 1994 and announce that the World Series was being canceled because of a players' strike.

While Selig's focus changed with his commissioner duties, his daily life did not. A creature of habit if there ever was one, Selig set up shop as commissioner in downtown Milwaukee, refusing to move to New York to work out of that long-established office. He continued to eat his standard, modest lunch—hot dog smothered in ketchup and a Diet Coke—at Gilles, a landmark frozen custard stand not far from Miller Park. Customers became accustomed to seeing the multitasking Selig, sitting in his car, eating his everyman fare, reading the sports pages, and conducting business over the telephone. And he still could be found nearly every Friday morning at Tony Lococo's Hair World, getting his weekly haircut.

Sentimental to a fault, Selig's passion for the game prompted him to initiate major changes he felt were necessary to prosper in an

TRIVIA

The Brewers have retired the numbers of only four players in franchise history. Who are they?

Answers to the trivia questions are on page 147.

ever-changing world. Refusing to yield to critics, he pushed forward with innovations such as the three-division format, wild-card playoff berths, interleague play, a comprehensive drug testing policy, and, most important for the growth of the game, revenue sharing among clubs. Many who demeaned Selig as a small-time former car salesman who was in over his head as commissioner soon were lauding him as a visionary.

"With revenue sharing, there's hope and faith in a lot of places now, including Milwaukee," said Selig, who understood the plight of small-market clubs from his years of trying to keep the Brewers afloat. "We changed the economic landscape of the sport beyond what anybody could have thought."

The reality of change struck closer to home for Selig and his family in 2004 when the Brewers were sold to Los Angeles investor Mark Attanasio. The Seligs had been involved in owning and operating the club since Day 1 in 1970, but he realized it was "time to go."

"I'll always have great memories of my years with the team," he said. "I'll always have a soft spot in my heart for the Brewers. Our group stayed together for nearly 40 years. That's amazing, when you think about it. I don't think you'll ever see that happen again.

"It was the right thing to do but I was still very emotional. In the end, the thing I thought about was that for a kid who walked the streets heartbroken in '64 (after the Braves decided to leave Milwaukee), it was a great ride."

ANSWERS TO
TRIVIA QUESTIONS

Page 2: Lew Krausse.

Page 10: The Chicago Cubs.

Page 11: 1955 and 1975.

Page 14: Cleveland's Jose Mesa.

Page 22: Detroit's Dave Roberts allowed a single by Aaron—his 3,771st career hit—on October 3, 1976, at County Stadium.

Page 31: Third baseman Don Money in 1978. Outfielder Larry Hisle and pitcher Lary Sorensen also were named to the AL squad that year.

Page 34: Robert Leroy Rodgers.

Page 41: 210 hits, 367 total bases, .578 slugging percentage, 46 doubles.

Page 47: Dwight Bernard and Jim Slaton.

Page 51: Sutton went 4–1 in those seven starts.

Page 58: Ted Simmons, with two.

Page 64: Shortstop Dale Sveum.

Page 70: Uecker played TV sportscaster George Owens.

Page 76: Boston's Jim Rice.

Page 78: Bill Parsons, with 13 in 1972.

Page 87: Billy Jo Robidoux, who played in only 23 games that season before undergoing knee surgery.

Page 92: Cecil Cooper.

Page 99: Odell Jones.

Page 105: Cleveland's Kenny Lofton.

Page 111: Graeme Lloyd.

Page 117: Hank Greenberg and Stan Musial (both at first base and the outfield).

Page 122: Cincinnati first baseman Sean Casey.

Page 129: The Kansas City Royals.

Page 140: Willie Mays (24 years, 137 days), with his 50th home run coming on September 20, 1955.

Page 145: Hank Aaron (No. 44), Rollie Fingers (No. 34), Robin Yount (No. 19), and Paul Molitor (No. 4).

The Milwaukee Brewers All-Time Roster (Through 2007 Season)

Players who have appeared in at least one game with the Milwaukee Brewers. The roster includes the Seattle Pilots of 1969.

A

Hank Aaron (OF)	1975–76
Jim Abbott (P)	1998–99
Juan Acevedo (P)	2000
Mike Adams (P)	2004–06
Joel Adamson (P)	1997
Jim Adduci (OF)	1986–88
Jack Aker (P)	1969
Izzy Alcantara (OF)	2002
Jay Aldrich (P)	1987–88
Andy Allanson (C)	1992
Hank Allen (OF)	1970
Felipe Alou (OF)	1974
Max Alvis (3B)	1970
Larry Anderson (P)	1974–75
Drew Anderson (OF)	2006
Greg Aquino (P)	2007
Rick Auerbach (SS)	1971–73
Don August (P)	1988–91
Jerry Augustine (P)	1975–84
Rick Austin (P)	1975–76
Jim Austin (P)	1991–93
Joe Azcue (C)	1972

B

Paul Bako (C)	2002
Dave Baldwin (P)	1970
Grant Balfour (P)	2007
Sal Bando (3B)	1977–81
Dick Baney (P)	1969
Brian Banks (1B)	1996–99
Steve Barber (P)	1969
Len Barker (P)	1987
Kevin Barker (1B)	1999–2000
Chris Barnwell (SS)	2006
Kevin Bass (OF)	1982
Dick Bates (P)	1969
Billy Bates (2B)	1989–90
Gary Beare (P)	1976–77
Larry Bearnarth (P)	1971
Rich Becker (OF)	1999
Andy Beene (P)	1983–84
Gary Bell (P)	1969
Jerry Bell (P)	1971–74
Juan Bell (2B)	1993
David Bell (3B)	2006
Ronnie Belliard (2B)	1998–2002
Jeff Bennett (P)	2004
Gary Bennett (C)	2004
Jason Bere (P)	1999–2000
Dwight Bernard (P)	1981–82
Sean Berry (3B)	1999–2000
Ken Berry (OF)	1974
Kurt Bevacqua (3B)	1975–76
Tommy Bianco (3B)	1975
Dante Bichette (OF)	1991–92
Mike Birkbeck (P)	1986–89
Henry Blanco (C)	2000–01

Mike Boddicker (P)	1993	Robinson Cancel (C)	1999
Dan Boitano (P)	1979–80	Tom Candiotti (P)	1983–84
Bobby Bolin (P)	1970	Mike Capel (P)	1990
Mark Bomback (P)	1978	Jose Capellan (P)	2005–07
Ricky Bones (P)	1992–96	Chris Capuano (P)	2004–07
Chris Bosio (P)	1986–92	Bernie Carbo (OF)	1976
Thad Bosley (OF)	1981	Jose Cardenal (OF)	1971
Ricky Bottalico (P)	2005	Cris Carpenter (P)	1996
Jim Bouton (P)	1969	Chuck Carr (OF)	1996–97
Steve Bowling (OF)	1976	Matias Carrillo (OF)	1991
Marshall Boze (P)	1996	Raul Casanova (C)	2000–02
Gene Brabender (P)	1969–70	Juan Castillo (2B)	1986–89
Glenn Braggs (OF)	1986–90	Bill Castro (P)	1974–80
Bucky Brandon (P)	1969	Rick Cerone (C)	1986
Russell Branyan (3B)	2004–05	Bill Champion (P)	1973–76
Ryan Braun (3B)	2007	Matt Childers (P)	2002
Ken Brett (P)	1972	Bobby Chouinard (P)	1997–98
Johnny Briggs (OF)	1971–75	Ryan Christenson (OF)	2001–02
Pete Broberg (P)	1975–76	Mark Ciardi (P)	1987
Greg Brock (1B)	1987–91	Jeff Cirillo (3B)	1994–99, 2005–06
Jeff Bronkey (P)	1994–95	Ron Clark (3B)	1969–72
Mark Brouhard (OF)	1980–85	Bobby Clark (OF)	1984–85
Kevin Brown (P)	1990–91	Brady Clark (OF)	2003–06
Kevin Brown (C)	2000–01	Royce Clayton (SS)	2003
Ollie Brown (OF)	1972–73	Mark Clear (P)	1986–88
Bruce Brubaker (P)	1970	Reggie Cleveland (P)	1979–81
Tom Brunansky (OF)	1993–94	Bryan Clutterbuck (P)	1986–89
George Brunet (P)	1969	Jaime Cocanower (P)	1983–86
Jim Bruske (P)	2000	Jim Colborn (P)	1972–76
Steve Brye (OF)	1977	Lou Collier (SS)	1999–2001
Mike Buddie (P)	2000–02	Bob Coluccio (OF)	1973–75
Dave Burba (P)	2003–04	Wayne Comer (OF)	1969–70
Bob Burda (1B)	1970	Billy Conigliaro (OF)	1972
Jeromy Burnitz (OF)	1996–2001	Jason Conti (OF)	2003
Ray Burris (P)	1985–87	Mike Coolbaugh (3B)	2001
Terry Burrows (P)	1996	Cecil Cooper (1B)	1977–87
Dave Bush (P)	2006–07	Rocky Coppinger (P)	1999–2001
		Francisco Cordero (P)	2006–07
C		Barry Cort (P)	1977
		Craig Counsell (2B)	2004, 2007
Jose Cabrera (P)	2002	Joe Crawford (P)	2000
Mike Caldwell (P)	1977–84	Chuck Crim (P)	1987–91
George Canale (1B)	1989–91		

Mike Crudale (P)	2003
Enrique Cruz (SS)	2003
Nelson Cruz (OF)	2005
Will Cunnane (P)	2000–01
Lafayette Currence (P)	1975

D

Jeff D'Amico (P)	1996–2002
Carl Dale (P)	1999
Danny Darwin (P)	1985–86
Bobby Darwin (OF)	1975–76
Mark Davis (P)	1997
Kane Davis (P)	2000, 2005
Doug Davis (P)	2003–06
Tommy Davis (OF)	1969
Brock Davis (OF)	1972
Dick Davis (OF)	1977–80
Jorge De La Rosa (P)	2004–06
Valerio De Los Santos (P)	1998–2003
Mike DeJean (P)	2001–03
Rob Deer (OF)	1986–90
Chris Demaria (P)	2006
Rick Dempsey (C)	1991
Elmer Dessens (P)	2007
Eddy Diaz (2B)	1997
Edgar Diaz (SS)	1986–90
Alex Diaz (OF)	1992–94
Rob Dibble (P)	1995
Ben Diggins (P)	2002
Joe Dillon (2B)	2007
Frank DiPino (P)	1981
John Donaldson (2B)	1969
Bill Doran (2B)	1993
Al Downing (P)	1970
Todd Dunn (OF)	1996–97
Jayson Durocher (P)	2002–03
Trent Durrington (2B)	2004–05

E

Jamie Easterly (P)	1981–83
Angel Echevarria (OF)	2000–01
Tom Edens (P)	1990

Bill Edgerton (P)	1969
Marshall Edwards (OF)	1981–83
Cal Eldred (P)	1991–99
Rob Ellis (OF)	1971–75
Dick Ellsworth (P)	1970–71
Narciso Elvira (P)	1990
Dave Engle (C)	1989
Matt Erickson (2B)	2004
Horacio Estrada (P)	1999–2000
Johnny Estrada (C)	2007
Leo Estrella (P)	2003
Andy Etchebarren (C)	1978
Dana Eveland (P)	2005–06

F

Jorge Fabregas (C)	2002
Steve Falteisek (P)	1999–2000
Ed Farmer (P)	1978
Mike Felder (OF)	1985–90
John Felske (C)	1972–73
Jared Fernandez (P)	2006
Tony Fernandez (SS)	2001
Mike Ferraro (3B)	1969–72
Mike Fetters (P)	1992–97
Prince Fielder (1B)	2005–07
Nelson Figueroa (P)	2002
Tom Filer (P)	1988–90
Rollie Fingers (P)	1981–85
Scott Fletcher (SS)	1992
John Flinn (P)	1980
Bryce Florie (P)	1996–97
Rich Folkers (P)	1977
Matt Ford (P)	2003
Ben Ford (P)	2004
Tony Fossas (P)	1989–90
Ray Fosse (C)	1979
John Foster (P)	2003
Chad Fox (P)	1998–2002
Julio Franco (DH)	1997
Terry Francona (1B)	1989–90
Tito Francona (OF)	1970
Wayne Franklin (P)	2002–03

La Vel Freeman (DH)	1989	Brian Harper (C)	1994
Danny Frisella (P)	1976	Tommy Harper (OF)	1969–71
Miguel Fuentes (P)	1969	Reggie Harris (P)	1998–99
		Vic Harris (2B)	1980
G		Lenny Harris (3B)	2002
Bob Galasso (P)	1979	Corey Hart (OF)	2004–07
Yovani Gallardo (P)	2007	Paul Hartzell (P)	1984
Gus Gandarillas (P)	2001–02	Tom Hausman (P)	1975–76
Jim Gantner (2B)	1976–92	Charlie Hayes (3B)	2000
Ramon Garcia (P)	1996	Jimmy Haynes (P)	2000–01
Pedro Garcia (2B)	1973–76	Neal Heaton (P)	1992
Rob Gardner (P)	1973	Mike Hegan (1B)	1969–77
John Gelnar (P)	1969–71	Jack Heidemann (SS)	1976–77
Chris George (P)	1991	Bob Heise (SS)	1971–73
Bob Gibson (P)	1983–86	Rick Helling (P)	2005–06
Gus Gil (2B)	1969–71	Wes Helms (3B)	2003–05
Brian Giles (2B)	1985	Rod Henderson (P)	1998–99
Keith Ginter (2B)	2002–04	Ben Hendrickson (P)	2004–07
Brian Givens (P)	1995–96	Doug Henry (P)	1991–94
Gary Glover (P)	2004–05	Adrian Hernandez (P)	2004
Geremi Gonzalez (P)	2006	Jose Hernandez (SS)	2000–02
Greg Goossen (1B)	1969–70	Mike Hershberger (OF)	1970
Jim Gosger (OF)	1969	Teddy Higuera (P)	1985–94
Tony Graffanino (2B)	2006–07	Sam Hinds (P)	1977
Charlie Greene (C)	1999	Larry Hisle (OF)	1978–82
Ben Grieve (OF)	2004	Fred Holdsworth (P)	1980
Marquis Grissom (OF)	1998–2000	Darren Holmes (P)	1990–92
Gabe Gross (OF)	2006–07	Paul Householder (OF)	1985–86
Tony Gwynn (OF)	2006–07	Tyler Houston (3B)	2000–02
		Steve Hovley (OF)	1969–70
H		Wilbur Howard (OF)	1973
Moose Haas (P)	1976–85	Roy Howell (3B)	1981–84
Bill Hall (SS)	2002–07	Joe Hudson (P)	1998
Bob Hamelin (DH)	1998	Bobby Hughes (C)	1998–99
Darryl Hamilton (OF)	1988–95	David Hulse (OF)	1995–96
Jeffrey Hammonds (OF)	2001–03	Bob Humphreys (P)	1970
Larry Haney (C)	1969, 1977–78	Jim Hunter (P)	1991
Jim Hannan (P)	1971	Dave Huppert (C)	1985
Greg Hansell (P)	1997	Jeff Huson (SS)	1997
Bob Hansen (DH)	1974–76		
J.J. Hardy (SS)	2005–07	**I**	
Pete Harnisch (P)	1997	Mike Ignasiak (P)	1991–95

J

Zach Jackson (P)	2006
Darrin Jackson (OF)	1997–98
John Jaha (1B)	1992–98
Dion James (OF)	1983–85
Geoff Jenkins (OF)	1998–2007
Marcus Jensen (C)	1998, 2002
John Henry Johnson (P)	1986–87
Mark Johnson (C)	2004
Deron Johnson (1B)	1974
Tim Johnson (SS)	1973–78
Doug Jones (P)	1982, 1996–98
Odell Jones (P)	1988
Chris Jones (OF)	2000
Von Joshua (OF)	1976–77
Jeff Juden (P)	1997–98

K

Scott Karl (P)	1995–99
Rickey Keeton (P)	1980–81
John Kennedy (3B)	1969–70
Jim Kern (P)	1984–85
Mark Kiefer (P)	1993–96
Steve Kiefer (3B)	1986–88
Brooks Kieschnick (P)	2003–04
Ray King (P)	2000–02, 2007
Matt Kinney (P)	2003–04
Ed Kirkpatrick (OF)	1977
Joe Kmak (C)	1993
Mark Knudson (P)	1986–91
Kevin Kobel (P)	1973–76
Pete Koegel (C)	1970–71
Brandon Kolb (P)	2000–01
Dan Kolb (P)	2003–06
Brad Komminsk (OF)	1987
Andy Kosco (OF)	1971
Corey Koskie (3B)	2006
Kevin Koslofski (OF)	1996
Lew Krausse (P)	1970–71
Ray Krawczyk (P)	1989
Bill Krueger (P)	1989–90

Dave Krynzel (OF)	2004–05
Ted Kubiak (2B)	1970–71
Art Kusnyer (C)	1976

L

Pete Ladd (P)	1982–85
Joe Lahoud (OF)	1972–73
Tom Lampkin (C)	1993
Dave LaPoint (P)	1980
George Lauzerique (P)	1970
Jack Lazorko (P)	1984
Tim Leary (P)	1985–86
Mark Lee (P)	1990–91
Carlos Lee (OF)	2005–06
Justin Lehr (P)	2005–06
Mark Leiter (P)	2001
Jeffrey Leonard (OF)	1988
Randy Lerch (P)	1981–82
Curtis Leskanic (P)	2000–03
Brad Lesley (P)	1985
Jesse Levis (C)	1996–98, 2001
Allen Levrault (P)	2000–02
Sixto Lezcano (OF)	1974–80
Jeff Liefer (OF)	2004
Jack Lind (SS)	1974–75
Scott Linebrink (P)	2007
Frank Linzy (P)	1972–73
Pedro Liriano (P)	2004
Pat Listach (SS)	1992–96
Graeme Lloyd (P)	1993–96
Bob Locker (P)	1969–70
Skip Lockwood (P)	1969–73
Doug Loman (OF)	1984–85
Jim Lonborg (P)	1972
Marcelino Lopez (P)	1971
Luis Lopez (SS)	2000–02
Mark Loretta (2B)	1995–2002
Andrew Lorraine (P)	2002
Willie Lozado (3B)	1984
Matt Luke (OF)	1999–2000
Gordy Lund (SS)	1969

M

Chris Mabeus (P)	2006
Julio Machado (P)	1990–91
Robert Machado (C)	2002
Alex Madrid (P)	1987
Chris Magruder (OF)	2004–05
Carlos Maldonado (P)	1993
Candy Maldonado (OF)	1991
Brian Mallette (P)	2002
Sean Maloney (P)	1997
David Manning (P)	2003
Rick Manning (OF)	1983–87
Josias Manzanillo (P)	1993
Mike Marshall (P)	1969
Luis Martinez (P)	2003
Buck Martinez (C)	1978–80
Greg Martinez (OF)	1998
Tom Matchick (SS)	1971
Mike Matheny (C)	1994–98
Mike Matthews (P)	2002
Dave May (OF)	1970–74, 1978
Derrick May (OF)	1995
Matt Maysey (P)	1993
Jamie McAndrew (P)	1995–97
Seth McClung (P)	2007
Bob McClure (P)	1977–86
Ben McDonald (P)	1996–97
Tim McIntosh (C)	1990–93
Ken McMullen (3B)	1977
Jerry McNertney (C)	1969–70
Doc Medich (P)	1982
Kevin Mench (OF)	2006–07
Jose Mercedes (P)	1994–98
Bob Meyer (P)	1969–70
Joey Meyer (DH)	1988–89
Matt Mieske (OF)	1992–97
Roger Miller (P)	1974
Damian Miller (C)	2005–07
Don Mincher (1B)	1969
Paul Mirabella (P)	1987–90
Angel Miranda (P)	1993–97
Mike Misuraca (P)	1997

Paul Mitchell (P)	1979–80
Bobby Mitchell (OF)	1971–75
Chad Moeller (C)	2004–06
Paul Molitor (DH)	1978–92
Don Money (3B)	1973–83
Donnie Moore (P)	1981
Charlie Moore (C)	1973–86
John Morris (P)	1969–71
Julio Mosquera (C)	2005
Curt Motton (OF)	1972
Lyle Mouton (OF)	1999–2000
James Mouton (OF)	2000–01
Willie Mueller (P)	1978–81
Greg Mullins (P)	1998
Tom Murphy (P)	1974–76
Tony Muser (1B)	1978
Mike Myers (P)	1998–99

N

Shane Nance (P)	2002–03
Jaime Navarro (P)	1989–94, 2000
Nick Neugebauer (P)	2001–04
Marc Newfield (OF)	1996–98
Ray Newman (P)	1972–73
Juan Nieves (P)	1986–88
Dave Nilsson (C)	1992–99
Laynce Nix (OF)	2006–07
Hideo Nomo (P)	1999
Takahito Nomura (P)	2002
Tim Nordbrook (SS)	1978–79
Rafael Novoa (P)	1993
Edwin Nunez (P)	1991–92

O

Wes Obermueller (P)	2003–05
Charlie O'Brien (C)	1987–90
Syd O'Brien (3B)	1972
Alex Ochoa (OF)	1999–2002
John O'Donoghue (P)	1969–70
Ben Oglivie (OF)	1978–86
Tomo Ohka (P)	2005–06
Jim Olander (OF)	1991

Troy O'Leary (OF)	1993–94	Dennis Powell (P)	1990
Joe Oliver (C)	1995	Bill Pulsipher (P)	1998–99
Jesse Orosco (P)	1991–94		
Pat Osburn (P)	1975	**Q**	
Keith Osik (C)	2003	Ruben Quevedo (P)	2001–03
Jimmy Osting (P)	2002	Jamie Quirk (C)	1977
Lyle Overbay (1B)	2004–05		
Eric Owens (OF)	1998	**R**	
Ray Oyler (SS)	1969	Hector Ramirez (P)	1999–2000
		Willie Randolph (2B)	1991
P		Merritt Ranew (C)	1969
Jim Paciorek (1B)	1987	Paul Ratliff (C)	1971–72
Jim Pagliaroni (C)	1969	Lance Rautzhan (P)	1979
Lance Painter (P)	2001	Randy Ready (2B)	1983–86
Dave Parker (OF)	1990	Kevin Reimer (OF)	1993
Manny Parra (P)	2007	Andy Replogle (P)	1978–79
Bill Parsons (P)	1971–73	Jerry Reuss (P)	1989
Bronswell Patrick (P)	1998	Al Reyes (P)	1995–99
Marty Pattin (P)	1969–71	Bob Reynolds (P)	1971
David Pember (P)	2002–03	Archie Reynolds (P)	1972
Elvis Pena (2B)	2001	Ken Reynolds (P)	1973
Roberto Pena (SS)	1970–71	Tommie Reynolds (OF)	1972
Eddie Perez (C)	2003	Paul Rigdon (P)	2000–01
Santiago Perez (SS)	2000	Ron Rightnowar (P)	1995
Danny Perez (OF)	1996	Ernest Riles (SS)	1985–88
Robert Perez (OF)	2001	Todd Ritchie (P)	2003
Jeff Peterek (P)	1989	Mike Rivera (C)	2006–07
Ray Peters (P)	1970	Sid Roberson (P)	1995
Kyle Peterson (P)	1999–2001	Billy Jo Robidoux (1B)	1985–88
Travis Phelps (P)	2004	Ron Robinson (P)	1990–92
Tommy Phelps (P)	2005	Eduardo Rodriguez (P)	1973–78
Rob Picciolo (SS)	1982–83	Ellie Rodriguez (C)	1971–73
Jim Pittsley (P)	1999	Garry Roggenburk (P)	1969
Dan Plesac (P)	1986–92	Rich Rollins (3B)	1969–70
Eric Plunk (P)	1998–99	Ed Romero (SS)	1977–85, 1989
Scott Podsednik (OF)	2003–04	Phil Roof (C)	1970–71
John Poff (OF)	1980	Rafael Roque (P)	1998–2000
Gus Polidor (SS)	1989–90	Jimmy Rosario (OF)	1976
Carlos Ponce (1B)	1985	Vinny Rottino (3B)	2006–07
Chuck Porter (P)	1981–85	Bruce Ruffin (P)	1992
Darrell Porter (C)	1971–76	Glendon Rusch (P)	2002–03
Mike Potts (P)	1996	Jim Rushford (OF)	2002

Gary Ryerson (P)	1972–73	Bill Spiers (SS)	1989–94
		Junior Spivey (2B)	2004–05
S		Ed Sprague (P)	1973–76
Ray Sadecki (P)	1976	Chris Spurling (P)	2006–07
Chris Saenz (P)	2004	Matt Stairs (OF)	2002
Lenn Sakata (2B)	1977–79	Steve Stanicek (DH)	1987
Alex Sanchez (OF)	2001–03	Fred Stanley (SS)	1969–70
Ken Sanders (P)	1970–72	Dave Stapleton (P)	1987–88
Julio Santana (P)	2005	Randy Stein (P)	1978
Victor Santos (P)	2004–05	Jerry Stephenson (P)	1969
Dennis Sarfate (P)	2006	Earl Stephenson (P)	1972
Ted Savage (OF)	1970–71	Mitch Stetter (P)	2007
Bob Scanlan (P)	1994–95, 2000	Kelly Stinnett (C)	1996–97
Dick Schofield (SS)	1971	Mel Stocker (OF)	2007
Bill Schroeder (C)	1983–88	Franklin Stubbs (1B)	1991–92
George Scott (1B)	1972–76	Everett Stull (P)	2000–02
Ray Searage (P)	1984–86	William Suero (2B)	1992–93
Bob Sebra (P)	1990	Jim Sundberg (C)	1984
Diego Segui (P)	1969	Jeff Suppan (P)	2007
Kevin Seitzer (3B)	1992–96	B.J. Surhoff (OF)	1987–95
Dick Selma (P)	1974	Gary Sutherland (2B)	1976
Richie Sexson (1B)	2000–03	Don Sutton (P)	1982–84
Bill Sharp (OF)	1975–76	Mac Suzuki (P)	2001
Ben Sheets (P)	2001–07	Dale Sveum (SS)	1986–91
Gary Sheffield (3B)	1988–92	Mark Sweeney (OF)	2000–01
Bob Sheldon (2B)	1974–77		
Chris Short (P)	1973	**T**	
Brian Shouse (P)	2006–07	Fred Talbot (P)	1969
Ted Simmons (C)	1981–85	Jim Tatum (1B)	1992
Allan Simpson (P)	2006	Chuck Taylor (P)	1972
Dick Simpson (OF)	1969	Tom Tellmann (P)	1983–84
Duane Singleton (OF)	1994–95	Frank Tepedino (1B)	1971
Bob Skube (OF)	1982–83	Ron Theobald (2B)	1971–72
Jim Slaton (P)	1971–77, 1979–83	Mike Thomas (P)	1995
Joe Slusarski (P)	1995	Gorman Thomas (OF)	1973–83, 1986
Travis Smith (P)	1998–2001	Dan Thomas (OF)	1976–77
Bernie Smith (OF)	1970–71	Ryan Thompson (OF)	2001–02
Mark Smith (OF)	2003	Dickie Thon (SS)	1993
John Snyder (P)	2000	Gary Timberlake (P)	1969
Russ Snyder (OF)	1970	Bill Travers (P)	1974–80
Lary Sorensen (P)	1977–80	Derrick Turnbow (P)	2005–07
Steve Sparks (P)	1995–96	Wayne Twitchell (P)	1970

U

Tim Unroe (1B)	1995–97

V

Sandy Valdespino (OF)	1969–70
Jose Valentin (SS)	1992–99
Dave Valle (C)	1994
Tim Van Egmond (P)	1996, 1998–99
John Vander Wal (OF)	2003
Claudio Vargas (P)	2007
Greg Vaughn (OF)	1989–96
Carlos Velazquez (P)	1973
Freddie Velazquez (C)	1969
Randy Veres (P)	1989–90
Jose Vidal (OF)	1969
Carlos Villanueva (P)	2006–07
Ron Villone (P)	1996–97
Fernando Vina (2B)	1995–99
Luis Vizcaino (P)	2002–04
Jack Voigt (OF)	1997
Bill Voss (OF)	1971–72
Pete Vuckovich (P)	1981–86
John Vukovich (3B)	1973–74

W

Paul Wagner (P)	1997–98
Rick Waits (P)	1983–85
Danny Walton (OF)	1969–71
Turner Ward (OF)	1993–96
David Weathers (P)	1990–2001
Floyd Weaver (P)	1971
Rickie Weeks (2B)	2003, 2005–07

Bill Wegman (P)	1985–95
Steve Whitaker (OF)	1969
Devon White (OF)	2001
Kevin Wickander (P)	1995–96
Floyd Wicker (OF)	1970–71
Bob Wickman (P)	1996–2000
Matt Williams (P)	1999–2000
Billy Williams (OF)	1969
Gerald Williams (OF)	1996–97
Antone Williamson (1B)	1997
Joe Winkelsas (P)	2006
Matt Wise (P)	2004–07
Jim Wohlford (OF)	1977–79
Dooley Womack (P)	1969
Brad Woodall (P)	1998
Steve Woodard (P)	1997–2000
Clyde Wright (P)	1974
Jamey Wright (P)	2000–02
Rick Wrona (C)	1994
Jimmy Wynn (OF)	1977

Y

Al Yates (OF)	1971
Ned Yost (C)	1980–83
Eric Young (2B)	2002–03
Mike Young (OF)	1988
Robin Yount (SS)	1974–93
Jeff Yurak (OF)	1978

Z

Peter Zoccolillo (OF)	2003
Eddie Zosky (SS)	1999

Bibliography

Aaron, Hank, and Lonnie Wheeler. *I Had a Hammer: The Hank Aaron Story.* New York: HarperCollins, 1991.

Clines, Frank. "Brewers Keep Winning Streak Alive With Rally." *Milwaukee Journal Sentinel,* April 23, 1999.

———. "For Years, Yanks Were Brewers' Rivals." *Milwaukee Journal Sentinel,* August 6, 1999.

———. "Lezcano's Slam Capped Emotional Opener in 1980." *Milwaukee Journal Sentinel,* May 8, 1999.

———. "Selig's Dream Finally Took Field." *Milwaukee Journal Sentinel,* September 24, 1999.

Cunningham, Michael. "Time for a Change: Brewers' Awful Start Costs Lopez His Job." *Milwaukee Journal Sentinel,* April 19, 2002.

D'Amato, Gary. "Cooper's Redemption Sweet." *Milwaukee Journal Sentinel,* August 18, 2002.

———. "Dalton's Deals Made Brewers Better." *Milwaukee Journal Sentinel,* August 11, 2002.

———. "Paulie Not a Slacker." *Milwaukee Journal Sentinel,* August 13, 2002.

Flaherty, Tom. "Caldwell Bounces Cardinals." *Milwaukee Journal,* October 12, 1982.

———. "Cards Pull Fast One on The Brewers." *Milwaukee Journal,* October 15, 1982.

————. "Cards Walk on by Brewers." *Milwaukee Journal*, October 13, 1982.

————. "Last Call is a Sad One." *Milwaukee Journal*, October 20, 1982.

————. "One Victory Away from Ecstasy." *Milwaukee Journal*, October 17, 1982.

————. "Stuper Puts Brewer Bats in a Stupor." *Milwaukee Journal*, October 19, 1982.

Haudricourt, Tom. "A House on Fire." *Milwaukee Journal Sentinel*, May 10, 2007.

————. "A True Queen of Diamonds." *Milwaukee Journal Sentinel*, September 23, 2000.

————. "Braun, Present, Future, Gather in Brewers' Infield." *Milwaukee Journal Sentinel*, May 26, 2007.

————. "Fans to Walk All Over Gorman, 'Gumby.'" *Milwaukee Journal Sentinel*, June 22, 2004.

————. "Few Saw Aaron's Final Homer." *Milwaukee Journal Sentinel*, August 27, 1999.

————. "Finally Out of the Red." *Milwaukee Journal Sentinel*, October 1, 2005.

————. "Fortunes Sink as Competition Rises." *Milwaukee Journal Sentinel*, May 30, 2007.

————. "Four Cast into National Spotlight." *Milwaukee Journal Sentinel*, July 2, 2007.

————. "Kuenn Took Young Robin Under His Wing." *Milwaukee Journal Sentinel*, July 16, 1999.

————. "Legacy: Brewers Believe They Have Talent, Depth to Add a Link in Milwaukee's Championship Cycle." *Milwaukee Journal Sentinel*, April 1, 2007.

————. "Little Hits Led to Comeback Victory for 1981 Brewers." *Milwaukee Journal Sentinel*, May 14, 1999.

————. "Milwaukee's 'Kids' Maintain Their Focus, Go Out Swinging." *Milwaukee Journal Sentinel,* October 1, 2007.

————. "Molitor Hopes Fans Respond Positively to His Honor." *Milwaukee Journal Sentinel,* June 10, 1999.

————. "Molitor Left On Deck as Hitting Streak Ended." *Milwaukee Journal Sentinel,* June 11, 1999.

————. "Pressure Cooking Unseasoned Team." *Milwaukee Journal Sentinel,* August 19, 2007.

————. "Replacement Starter Cranks." *Milwaukee Journal Sentinel,* June 14, 2007.

————. "Roller Coaster Down." *Milwaukee Journal Sentinel,* June 18, 2007.

————. "Selig Rode Up Front on the Roller Coaster." *Milwaukee Journal Sentinel,* September 23, 2000.

————. "Stadium Opener Has a Perfect Ending to a Wonderful Start." *Milwaukee Journal Sentinel,* April 7, 2001.

————. "The Final 4: Brewers Retire Molitor's Number." *Milwaukee Journal Sentinel,* June 11, 1999.

————. "The Kid Makes It to the Hall of Fame." *Milwaukee Journal Sentinel,* January 5, 1999.

————. "Thomas' Hit Ties the Series." *Milwaukee Journal,* October 16, 1982.

————. "Yount's Rebel Act Became a Legend." *Milwaukee Journal Sentinel,* July 23, 1999.

Milwaukee Brewers. "History: Brewers History." Official Site of the Milwaukee Brewers. http://milwaukee.brewers.mlb.com/mil/history/index.jsp.

Olson, Drew. "Back in General Direction." *Milwaukee Journal Sentinel,* September 26, 2002.

————. "Brewers Turn to Braves for New GM." *Milwaukee Journal Sentinel,* September 21, 1999.

————. "For Molitor, This Hit Is Biggest of All." *Milwaukee Journal Sentinel,* January 6, 2004.

————. "Milwaukee Was So Close, Yet So Far." *Milwaukee Journal Sentinel,* September 3, 1999.

————. "Playing with the Big Boys: Talent Was Evident Early." *Milwaukee Journal Sentinel,* July 16, 1999.

————. "Today, Uecker Bats a Thousand." *Milwaukee Journal Sentinel,* July 27, 2003.

————. "Uecker's Standup Act Leaves 'Em Laughing." *Milwaukee Journal Sentinel,* July 27, 2003.

————. "Yount Sent Carew Home, Milwaukee to Series." *Milwaukee Journal Sentinel,* August 20, 1999.

Parrott, Harold. *The Lords of Baseball: A Wry Look at a Side of the Game the Fan Seldom Sees—The Front Office,* 2nd ed. Atlanta: Longstreet Press, 2002.

Van Lindt, Carson. *The Seattle Pilots Story.* New York City: Marabou Publishing, 1993.

Walker, Don. "Bamberger, 'Bombers' Brewed Team's 1st Winning Year." *Milwaukee Journal Sentinel,* April 6, 2004.

Walker, Don, and Gary D'Amato. "A Fan First." *Milwaukee Journal Sentinel,* April 2, 2001.

Walker, Don, and Drew Olson. "Brewers Replace Selig-Prieb, Taylor." *Milwaukee Journal Sentinel,* September 25, 2002.